Active Korean 2

Active Korean 2

서울대학교 언어교육원
Language Education Institute
Seoul National University

TWO PONDS
|주| 투판즈

Preface 머리말

Active Korean 2는 한국어 성인 학습자를 위한 단기 연수용(약 60시간) 한국어 교재 시리즈 중 둘째 권이다. 그동안 대부분의 한국어 교재는 집중 과정용으로 개발되어, 단기간에 실제적인 한국어 의사소통 능력을 키우고자 하는 학습자에게는 비효율적인 측면이 있었다. 이 책은 한국어를 처음 배우는 학습자들이 단기간에 기초적인 의사소통 능력을 갖추도록 하기 위해서 개발되었으며, 다음과 같은 특징을 가지고 있다.

첫째, 상황 및 기능 중심적 교수요목을 바탕으로 일상생활에서 사용하는 실제적이고 기본적인 내용으로 구성하였다. 초급 학습자들에게 필수적인 상황 및 기능을 중심으로 어휘와 문법, 표현을 선정하였다.

둘째, 체계적인 어휘 및 문법 학습이 이루어지도록 하였다. 매 과의 첫머리에 의미 범주와 품사별로 어휘 목록을 제시하고, 매 과의 마지막에 확장 표현 및 어휘를 제시하여 학습의 편의를 꾀하였다. 또한 문법 항목에 대한 자세한 설명을 통해 학습자가 문법을 정확하게 이해하여 적절하게 사용할 수 있도록 하였다.

셋째, 의사소통 기능을 통합적으로 활용하고 목표 문법을 완전히 습득하도록 하는 과제와 활동을 다양하게 제공하였다. 이러한 과제 수행을 통해 학습자는 유창성을 향상시키고 학습 의욕을 고취시킬 수 있다.

넷째, 수업의 구조와 학습자를 고려하여 단원 체제를 구성하였다. 주제와 상황에 맞는 문법과 표현, 그것을 활용한 간단한 대화, 확장된 담화의 순으로 제시함으로써 수업의 일반적 구조에 맞고 학습자의 이해와 활용이 용이하게 하였다.

다섯째, 본 교재에서는 어휘와 표현, 문법과 함께 듣기, 말하기, 읽기, 쓰기를 통합적으로 활용할 수 있는 능력을 기른다. 별도로 구성된 워크북을 통해서는 어휘 및 표현 연습과 문법 연습을 통해 학습 내용을 연습하고 정리해 볼 수 있다.

여섯째, 다양한 사진과 삽화 등 시각 자료를 풍부하게 제공하여 실제적이고 흥미 있는 학습이 가능하도록 하였다. 또한 시각 자료를 통해 의미와 상황을 정확하게 전달하고 학습자의 흥미를 유발함으로써 학습 효과를 높이고자 하였다.

일곱째, 수업용 교재로서뿐만 아니라 자율 학습용 교재로서도 사용이 가능하도록 배려하였다. 각 과에 제시된 순서대로 학습해 나가면 성공적인 학습 결과를 얻을 수 있도록 구성하였으며, 문법 설명과 지시문 등이 영어로 명료하게 제시되어 있다. 또한 학습 결과를 스스로 점검하고 확인할 수 있어 자기 평가가 가능하다.

이 책이 완성되기까지 오랜 기간에 걸쳐 집필 및 출판 과정에 헌신적으로 참여해 주신 교재개발위원회 선생님들, 번역을 맡아 주신 한국어교육센터의 함창덕 선생님, 현혜미 선생님, 번역 감수를 해 주신 외국어교육센터의 박준성 선생님의 노고에 이 자리를 빌려 깊은 감사를 드린다. 아울러 이 책이 출판되기까지 많은 도움을 주신 투판즈의 사장님과 편집진 여러분께도 감사의 마음을 전한다.

2006. 12.

김 성 규
서울대학교 언어교육원 한국어교육센터 소장

Active Korean 2 is the second volume in the Korean language textbook series designed for adult learners in a short-term training course (about 60 hours) of Korean language. Most textbooks of Korean language up until recently were developed for intensive courses, so they were not suitable for learners who wanted to improve their communication skills in a short period of time. Written for adult learners who are beginning to learn Korean as a foreign language, it aims to develop learners' basic communication skills in a short period of time by using the following methods:

First, on the basis of a situation and function centered syllabus, this book is composed of essential vocabulary, grammar and expressions for beginners derived from everyday situations and functions of real-life.

Second, this book aims to enable learners to acquire vocabulary and grammar systematically. To facilitate active vocabulary building, vocabulary lists, which are categorized by meanings and parts of speech, are presented on the first page of each unit, and extended vocabulary and expressions are presented at the end of each unit. Through the detailed explanation of grammar items, learners are able to understand the target grammar accurately and use it appropriately.

Third, various tasks and activities are provided to enable learners to acquire the target grammar and apply it to practical situations. Through these challenging tasks and activities, learners are able to improve their communicative competence.

Fourth, units are organized in consideration of class structure and learners. Grammar and expressions related to the topic and the given situations, a simple dialogue based on the topic and an extended conversation are presented in order in every unit to suit a general class structure and to facilitate learners' understanding and application.

Fifth, this book features integration of vocabulary, expressions, grammar, listening, speaking, reading and writing. The separate workbook helps learners to practice and organize what they have learned from the main textbook through exercises in grammar, expressions and vocabulary.

Sixth, a wide variety of photos and illustrations are provided to arouse learners' interests in learning and enable learners to have an accurate understanding of the given meanings and situations.

Seventh, this book can be used not only as a textbook for classes but also as a self-study book. Studying each unit in order will lead learners to successfully learn on one's own. To facilitate learners' understanding, explanations on grammar and instructions are presented in English, and self-assessment is possible as well.

We wish to express our sincere gratitude to all the instructors from the Textbook Development Committee who have contributed to the work of writing and publication of this book. We are also greatly indebted to Mr. Chang-Deok Hahm and Hae-mi Hyun from the Korean Language Education Center for editing the English translations, Mr. Joon-Sung Park from the Foreign Language Education Center for proofreading the translations. In addition, we would like to convey our gratitude to the CEO of TWOPONDS and his editorial staff for their generous support in having this volume published.

December 2006

Kim Seong Kyu

Director, Korean Language Education Center
Language Education Institute, Seoul National University

How to Use This Book 일러두기

This book consists of 9 units. Each unit consists of the following sections.

UNIT 1

Family

가족

In This Unit

- Using honorific expressions 존댓말로 말하기
- Introducing family members 가족 소개하기
- Talking about possessions 소유 관계 표현하기

16 UNIT 1

In This Unit

Objectives and functions to learn in each unit are presented in 'In This Unit.'

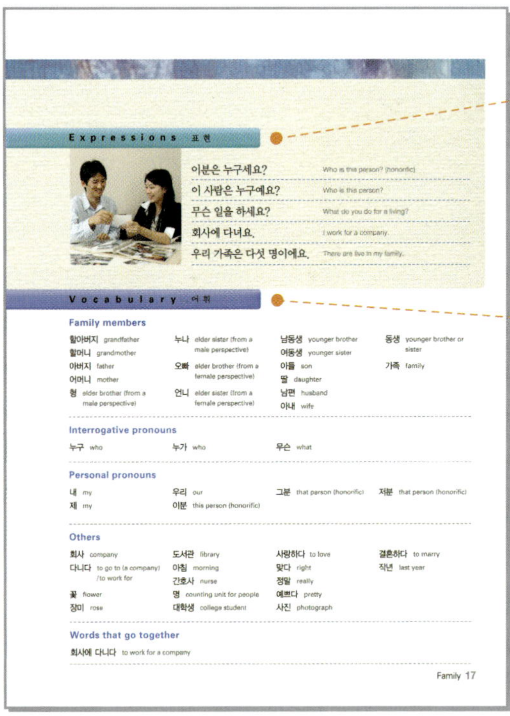
Expressions 표현

이분은 누구세요?	Who is this person? (honorific)
이 사람은 누구예요?	Who is this person?
무슨 일을 하세요?	What do you do for a living?
회사에 다녀요.	I work for a company.
우리 가족은 다섯 명이에요.	There are five in my family.

Vocabulary 어휘

Family members

할아버지 grandfather
할머니 grandmother
아버지 father
어머니 mother
형 elder brother (from a male perspective)
누나 elder sister (from a male perspective)
오빠 elder brother (from a female perspective)
언니 elder sister (from a female perspective)
남동생 younger brother
여동생 younger sister
아들 son
딸 daughter
남편 husband
아내 wife
동생 younger brother or sister
가족 family

Interrogative pronouns

누구 who
누가 who
무슨 what

Personal pronouns

내 my
제 my
우리 our
이분 this person (honorific)
그분 that person (honorific)
저분 that person (honorific)

Others

회사 company
다니다 to go to (a company) /to work for
꽃 flower
장미 rose
도서관 library
아침 morning
간호사 nurse
명 counting unit for people
대학생 college student
사랑하다 to love
맞다 right
정말 really
예쁘다 pretty
사진 photograph
결혼하다 to marry
작년 last year

Words that go together

회사에 다니다 to work for a company

Family 17

Expressions

The key expressions related to the topic and functions of each unit are presented in this section. These essential expressions for communication are presented in sentence unit.

Vocabulary

New vocabulary words that appear in each unit are presented in this section. Collocational expressions are categorized separately by 'Words that go together.' This 'Vocabulary' section will function as a dictionary for learners while studying each unit.

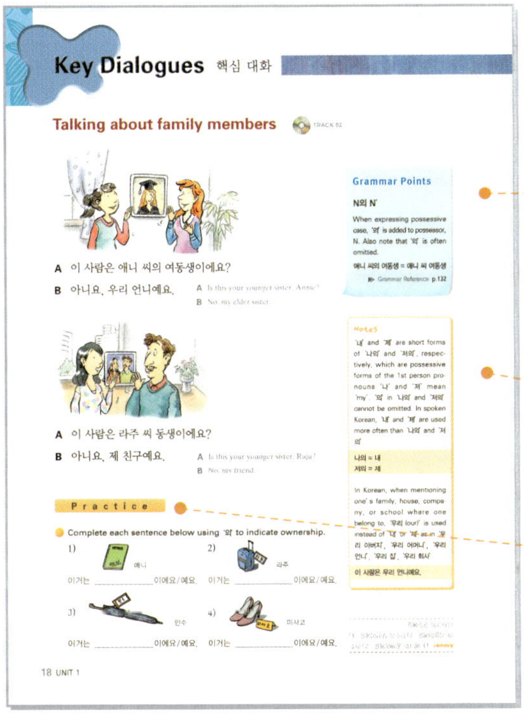

Key Dialogues 핵심 대화

Talking about family members

A 이 사람은 애니 씨의 여동생이에요?
B 아니요, 우리 언니예요.

A 이 사람은 라주 씨 동생이에요?
B 아니요, 제 친구예요.

Practice

Complete each sentence below using '의' to indicate ownership.

18 UNIT 1

Key Dialogues

This section introduces a few sets of a short dialogue and the grammar points.

Grammar Points

Key explanations on the new grammar points of each unit are presented. More explanations on the grammar are presented in 'Grammar Reference' at the end of this book.

Notes

Basic explanations on the essential vocabulary and expressions used in the dialogue are presented.

Practice

You can review what you have learned in 'Grammar Points' through various forms of exercises. The answers are presented upside down on the same page.

Conversation Drills 대화 연습

Conversation

A 진아 씨, 이분은 누구세요?
B 우리 아버지세요.
A 아버지는 무슨 일을 하세요?
B 은행에서 일하세요.

A 이 사람은 누구예요?
B 제 동생이에요.
A 동생은 뭘 해요?
B 학생이에요.

Check it

Practice the dialogue with your partner. Use the pictures below as cues.

22 UNIT 1

Conversation Drills

A couple of longer dialogues designed to allow learners to practice the sentences from 'Key Dialogues' are presented in this section. Role play using the drills at the bottom allows learners to practice the dialogue.

Check it

'Check it' enhances learners' comprehension of the dialogue.

How to Use This Book 일러두기

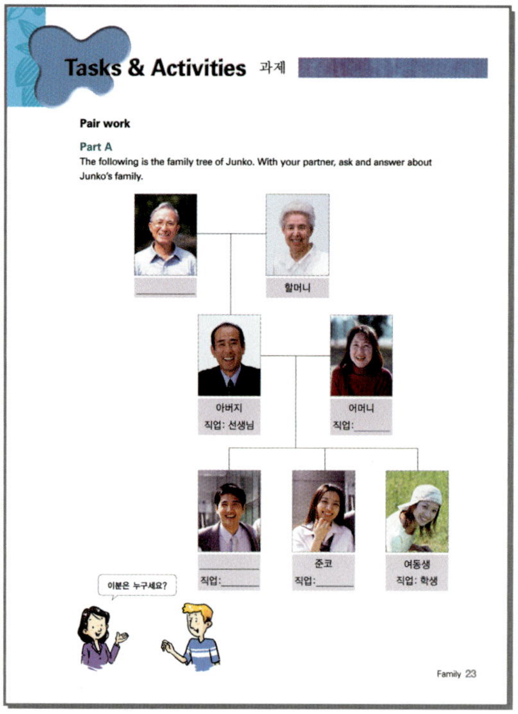

Tasks & Activities 과제

Pair work

Part A

The following is the family tree of Junko. With your partner, ask and answer about Junko's family.

할머니

아버지
직업: 선생님

어머니
직업: ______

직업: ______

준코
직업: ______

여동생
직업: 학생

이분은 누구세요?

Family 23

Tasks & Activities

Various tasks and activities in this section such as interviews and games are related to the topic and functions of each unit, and these tasks and activities make each lesson task-based and significant.

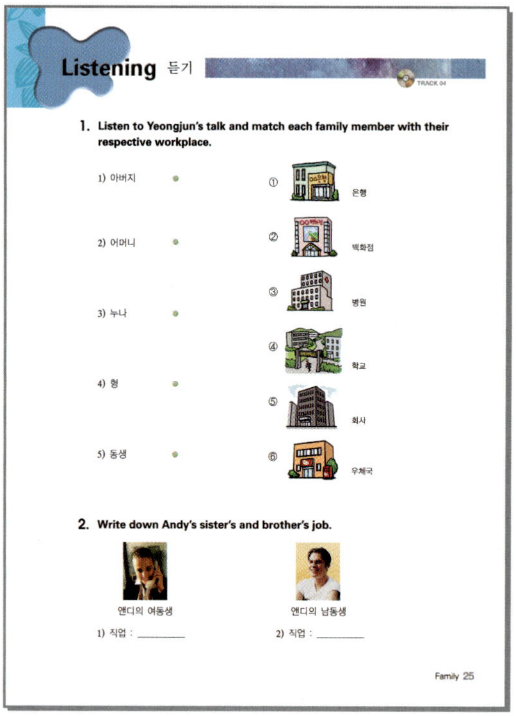

Listening 듣기

TRACK 04

1. Listen to Yeongjun's talk and match each family member with their respective workplace.

1) 아버지
2) 어머니
3) 누나
4) 형
5) 동생

① 은행
② 백화점
③ 병원
④ 학교
⑤ 회사
⑥ 우체국

2. Write down Andy's sister's and brother's job.

앤디의 여동생
1) 직업 : ______

앤디의 남동생
2) 직업 : ______

Family 25

Listening

This is a listening exercise covering grammar, vocabulary and expressions that are carried throughout each unit. The dialogue in this section is using authentic language in a wide range of settings to help learners prepare for real-life listening tasks.

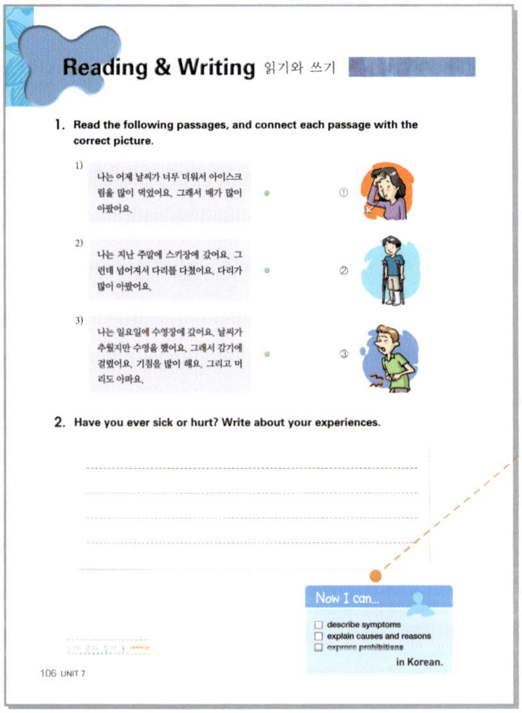
Reading & Writing 읽기와 쓰기

1. Read the following passages, and connect each passage with the correct picture.

1) 나는 어제 날씨가 너무 더워서 아이스크림을 많이 먹었어요. 그래서 배가 많이 아팠어요.

2) 나는 지난 주말에 스키장에 갔어요. 그런데 넘어져서 다리를 다쳤어요. 다리가 많이 아팠어요.

3) 나는 일요일에 수영장에 갔어요. 날씨가 추웠지만 수영을 했어요. 그래서 감기에 걸렸어요. 기침을 많이 해요. 그리고 머리도 아파요.

① ② ③

2. Have you ever sick or hurt? Write about your experiences.

Now I can...

- ☐ describe symptoms
- ☐ explain causes and reasons
- ☐ express prohibitions

in Korean.

106 UNIT 7

Reading & Writing

This section provides reading and writing practices through read-and-answer and read-and-write exercises to help learners understand the written language and improve their written expressions.

Now I can

Each unit ends with the opportunity for learners to wrap up what they have learned and assess their achievement of learning objectives.

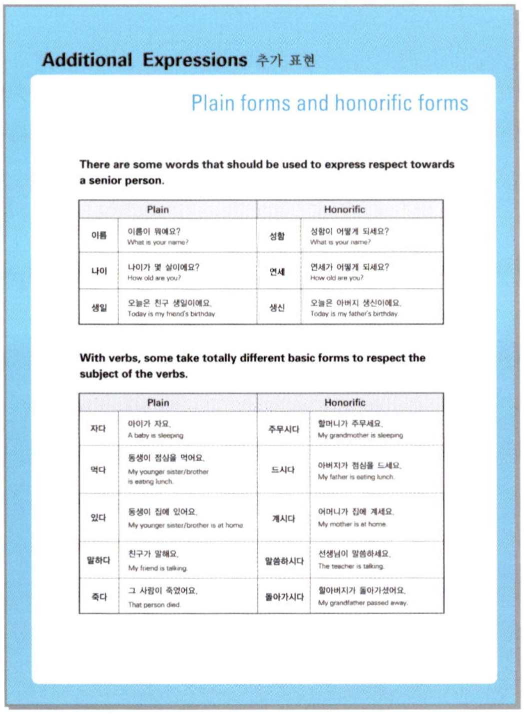
Additional Expressions 추가 표현

Plain forms and honorific forms

There are some words that should be used to express respect towards a senior person.

Plain		Honorific	
이름	이름이 뭐예요? What is your name?	성함	성함이 어떻게 되세요? What is your name?
나이	나이가 몇 살이에요? How old are you?	연세	연세가 어떻게 되세요? How old are you?
생일	오늘은 친구 생일이에요. Today is my friend's birthday	생신	오늘은 아버지 생신이에요. Today is my father's birthday

With verbs, some take totally different basic forms to respect the subject of the verbs.

Plain		Honorific	
자다	아이가 자요. A baby is sleeping	주무시다	할머니가 주무세요. My grandmother is sleeping
먹다	동생이 점심을 먹어요. My younger sister/brother is eating lunch.	드시다	아버지가 점심을 드세요. My father is eating lunch.
있다	동생이 집에 있어요. My younger sister/brother is at home	계시다	어머니가 집에 계세요. My mother is at home.
말하다	친구가 말해요. My friend is talking.	말씀하시다	선생님이 말씀하세요. The teacher is talking.
죽다	그 사람이 죽었어요. That person died.	돌아가시다	할아버지가 돌아가셨어요. My grandfather passed away.

Additional Expressions

Extended vocabulary words and expressions are presented with illustrations and photos. Although they are a little beyond the level of each unit, they are useful expressions for daily life.

How to Use This Book 일러두기

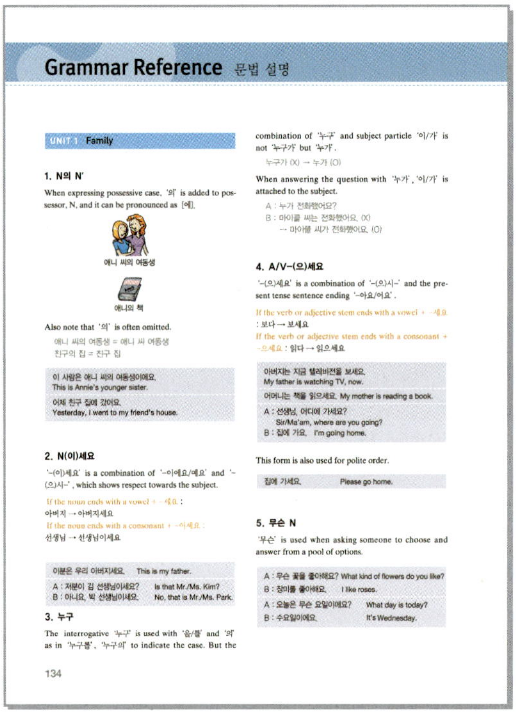

Grammar Reference

This section at the end of the book presents detailed explanations of 'Grammar Points' in each unit. Further explanations on grammar structures will be helpful for learners as well as instructors.

Glossary

It lists all the vocabulary words presented throughout the textbook and Grammar Reference with the meanings, and indicates the unit where they first appear.

Abbreviations in the book

N	noun	A	adjective
V	verb	S	sentence

Contents 차례

Scope and Sequence 교재 구성표

Unit	Expressions 표현	Vocabulary 어휘	Grammar 문법	Key Dialogues 핵심 대화
Unit 1 Family 가족	• Expressions related to introducing family members	• Family members • Interrogative pronouns • Personal pronouns	• N의 N′ • N(이)세요 • 누구 • A/V-(으)세요 • 무슨 N • A/V-(으)셨어요	• Talking about family members • Talking about one's seniors/elders
Unit 2 Transportation 교통	• Expressions related to transportation	• Means of transportation • Vocabulary related to transportation	• N에서 N′을/를 타다 • N에서 내리다 • N에서 N′(으)로 갈아타다 • N을/를 타고 가다/오다 • ‘ㄷ’ irregular verbs • V-아야/어야 되다	• Talking about transportation • Talking about how to get to somewhere • Talking about what one should do
Unit 3 Reason 이유	• Expressions needed when giving excuses	• Vocabulary related to reason • Languages • Musical instruments • Sports	• 못 V • A/V-아서/어서 • ‘ㅂ’ irregular adjectives • N(이)라서 • N(이)나 N′	• Talking about what one cannot or could not do • Giving a reason • Giving two or more alternatives
Unit 4 Post Office 우체국	• Expressions needed at the post office	• Vocabulary related to the post office • Continents & Countries • Term/Period	• V-(으)ㄹ 거예요 • N(으)로 • A/V-(으)면 • N한테	• Talking about future plans • Talking about means or methods • Telling what's inside • Talking about conditions • Indicating the receiver
Unit 5 Reservations 예약	• Expressions related to making reservations	• Vocabulary related to reservations	• V-(으)ㄹ 수 있다 • A-(으)ㄴ데요/V-는데요 • V-고 싶다 • N 동안 • N부터	• Talking about possibility or ability • Buying tickets • When expressing what one wants to do • Discussing length of time • Asking about something

Conversation Drills 대화 연습	Tasks & Activities 과제	Listening 듣기	Reading & Writing 읽기와 쓰기	Additional Expressions 추가 표현
• Introducing family members	• Talking about the relations of the family members	• Listening for one's family members' jobs • Listening for family relations	• Introducing family members and their jobs	• Plain forms and honorific forms
• Asking and answering how to get to somewhere • Asking and answering where to get off and how long it takes	• Explaining how to get home using public transportation	• Founding out how to get to a destination by subway • Understanding what one should do • Listening for the way and time to get to the destination	• Expressing how to get to a destination and how long it takes	• In a taxi • Types of trains in Korea
• Telling a reason • Making an appointment	• Making causal relation sentences	• Understanding a reason for turning down an offer • Understanding a reason after listening	• A passage with causal relation	• When apologizing • When showing gratitude
• Sending a parcel	• Telling what to do in each situation	• Understanding what to do in each situation • Understanding a dialogue at the post office	• A postcard sent from one's trip	• How to write the address on an envelope • Another way to count days
• Reserving an airplane ticket • Reserving a hotel room	• Discussing the age at which one can do a certain work in each country	• Understanding what one wants to do • Understanding a flight itinerary • Understanding details of a hotel reservation	• Writing an e-mail about one's trip itinerary and plans to meet up with a friend • Writing expressions needed to reserve an airplane ticket	• Types of tickets • Types of rooms according to the number of occupants • Changing a reservation and getting a refund for a ticket

Scope and Sequence 교재 구성표

Unit	Expressions 표현	Vocabulary 어휘	Grammar 문법	Key Dialogues 핵심 대화
Unit 6 Etiquette 예의	• Expressions related to etiquette • Expressions related to permission and agreement	• Vocabulary related to etiquette • Places • Emotion	• V-아도/어도 되다 • V-(으)면 안 되다 • A/V-(으)ㄹ 때	• Expressing permissions • Expressing prohibitions • Expressing a point of time
Unit 7 Hospital 병원	• Expressions used in a hospital	• Body • Symptom	• 'ㅡ' irregular verbs & adjectives • N이/가 아프다 • N도 • A/V-(으)니까 • V-지 마세요	• Explaining where it hurts • Explaining why one came to see the doctor • Describing symptoms • Giving a reason • Expressing prohibitions
Unit 8 Advice & Suggestions 충고와 제안	• Expressions of agreement • Expressions related to worries	• Vocabulary related to health • Vocabulary related to worries	• N은/는 N'한테 좋다/나쁘다 • N은/는 N'에 좋다/나쁘다 • V-아/어 보세요 • V-는 게 어때요? • 'ㄹ' irregular verbs & adjectives	• Asking for and giving advice • Making suggestions
Unit 9 Shopping 쇼핑	• Expressions related to shopping	• Vocabulary related to shopping • Colors	• A-(으)ㄴ N • S-고 S' • N을/를 N'(으)로 바꾸다 • N보다 (더) A • A-(으)ㄴ 거	• Buying something at a store • Recommending something • Exchanging • Comparing

Conversation Drills 대화 연습	Tasks & Activities 과제	Listening 듣기	Reading & Writing 읽기와 쓰기	Additional Expressions 추가 표현
• Asking for and giving permission • Talking about proper etiquettes in certain situations	• Asking and answering what is culturally acceptable and not in different countries	• Understanding what one should not do • Understanding what one may do • Finding out why something should not be done • Understanding what to do in a certain situation	• Understanding the regulations of a library • Writing the regulations for a dormitory	• Manners that should be kept in Korea
• Describing the symptoms and getting medical treatment	• Making a sentence using expressions which show reasons	• Listening to the expressions on prohibition • Listening for the symptoms • Listening to a dialogue in a hospital	• Writing after reading how one got hurt	• Symptoms
• Listening to someone's worries and giving advice	• Recommending what is famous and thus deserves boasting	• Giving advice • Listening to a conversation in a hospital	• Reading about someone's worries and then writing advice	• Situations where advice is needed
• Buying clothes • Exchanging what one bought	• Comparing	• Listening to comparative expressions • Listening to shopping situations	• Markets and department stores	• Expressions related to wearing

UNIT 1

Family
가족

In This Unit

- Using honorific expressions 존댓말로 말하기
- Introducing family members 가족 소개하기
- Talking about possessions 소유 관계 표현하기

Expressions 표현

이분은 누구세요?	Who is this person? (honorific)
이 사람은 누구예요?	Who is this person?
무슨 일을 하세요?	What do you do for a living?
회사에 다녀요.	I work for a company.
우리 가족은 다섯 명이에요.	There are five in my family.

Vocabulary 어휘

Family members

할아버지 grandfather
할머니 grandmother
아버지 father
어머니 mother
형 elder brother (from a male perspective)
누나 elder sister (from a male perspective)
오빠 elder brother (from a female perspective)
언니 elder sister (from a female perspective)
남동생 younger brother
여동생 younger sister
아들 son
딸 daughter
남편 husband
아내 wife
동생 younger brother or sister
가족 family

Interrogative pronouns

누구 who
누가 who
무슨 what

Personal pronouns

내 my
제 my
우리 our
이분 this person (honorific)
그분 that person (honorific)
저분 that person (honorific)

Others

회사 company
다니다 to go to (a company) /to work for
꽃 flower
장미 rose
도서관 library
아침 morning
간호사 nurse
명 counting unit for people
대학생 college student
사랑하다 to love
맞다 right
정말 really
사진 photograph
예쁘다 pretty
결혼하다 to marry
작년 last year

Words that go together

회사에 다니다 to work for a company

Key Dialogues 핵심 대화

Talking about family members

TRACK 02

A 이 사람은 애니 씨의 여동생이에요?

B 아니요, 우리 언니예요.

A Is this your younger sister, Annie?
B No, my elder sister.

A 이 사람은 라주 씨 동생이에요?

B 아니요, 제 친구예요.

A Is this your younger sister, Raju?
B No, my friend.

Grammar Points

N의 N′

When expressing possessive case, '의' is added to possessor, N. Also note that '의' is often omitted.

애니 씨의 여동생 = 애니 씨 여동생

▶ Grammar Reference p.134

Notes

'내' and '제' are short forms of '나의' and '저의', respectively, which are possessive forms of the 1st person pronouns '나' and '저' mean 'my'. '의' in '나의' and '저의' cannot be omitted. In spoken Korean, '내' and '제' are used more often than '나의' and '저의'.

나의 = 내
저의 = 제

In Korean, when mentioning one's family, house, company, or school where one belong to, '우리 (our)' is used instead of '내' or '제' as in '우리 아버지', '우리 어머니', '우리 언니', '우리 집', '우리 회사'.

이 사람은 우리 언니예요.

Practice

Complete each sentence below using '의' to indicate ownership.

1) 

애니

이거는 ______________이에요/예요.

2) 

라주

이거는 ______________이에요/예요.

3) 

민수

이거는 ______________이에요/예요.

4) 

미사코

이거는 ______________이에요/예요.

Answer 1) 애니의 공책이에요 2) 라주의 가방이에요 3) 민수의 우산이에요 4) 미사코의 구두예요

Talking about one's seniors/elders (1)

TRACK 02

A 이분은 누구세요?

B 우리 아버지세요.

A Who is this?

B My father.

Grammar Points

N(이)세요

'-(이)세요' is a combination of '-이에요/예요' and '-(으)시-', which shows respect towards the subject.

nouns ending with a vowel + -세요 : 아버지 → 아버지세요

nouns ending with a consonant + -이세요 : 선생님 → 선생님이세요

▶ Grammar Reference p.134

Practice

1 Circle the correct sentence ending.

1) 할아버지는 의사(세요 / 이세요).

2) 그분은 은행원(세요 / 이세요).

3) 어머니는 요리사(세요 / 이세요).

4) 할머니는 선생님(세요 / 이세요).

2 Choose the correct word from the box to complete each sentence.

누가 누구의 누구를

A 누가 전화했어요?
B 동생이 전화했어요.

1) A ________ 구두예요?
B 어머니의 구두예요.

2) A ________ 만났어요?
B 친구를 만났어요.

3) A ________ 왔어요?
B 친구가 왔어요.

4) A ________ 할아버지세요?
B 우리 할아버지세요.

Grammar Points

누구

The interrogative '누구' is used with '을/를' and '의' as in '누구를', '누구의' to indicate the case. But the combination of '누구' and subject particle '이/가' is not '누구가' but '누가'.

누구가 (X) → 누가 (O)

▶ Grammar Reference p.134

Answer 1 1) 세요 2) 이세요 3) 세요 4) 이세요 2 1) 누구의 2) 누구를 3) 누가 4) 누구의

Talking about one's seniors/elders (2)

TRACK 02

A 아버지는 뭘 하세요?

B 회사에 다니세요.

A What does your father do for a living?

B He works for a company.

A 어머니는 무슨 일을 하세요?

B 선생님이세요.

A What does your mother do for a living?

B She is a teacher.

Grammar Points

A/V-(으)세요

'-(으)세요' is a combination of '-(으)시-' and the present tense sentence ending '-아요/어요'.

verb or adjective stems ending with a vowel + -세요 :
보다 → 보세요

verb or adjective stems ending with a consonant + -으세요 : 읽다 → 읽으세요

▶ Grammar Reference p.134

Practice

1 Complete each sentence using the correct honorific ending.

가다
어머니가 시장에 가세요.

1) 
입다
어머니가 코트를 ____________.

2) 
사다
어머니가 구두를 ____________.

3) 
읽다
어머니가 신문을 ____________.

2 Complete each sentence below using '무슨'.

A 무슨 차를 마셔요?
B 녹차를 마셔요.

1) A ____________ 샀어요?
B 장미를 샀어요.

2) A ____________ 좋아해요?
B 사과를 좋아해요.

3) A ____________ 했어요?
B 수영을 했어요.

Grammar Points

무슨 N

'무슨' is used when asking someone to choose and answer from a pool of options.

무슨 책 읽어요?

▶ Grammar Reference p.134

Answer 1 1) 입으세요 2) 사세요 3) 읽으세요 2 1) 무슨 꽃을 2) 무슨 과일을 3) 무슨 운동을

Talking about one's seniors/elders (3)

TRACK 02

A 김 선생님은 어디에 가셨어요?

B 도서관에 가셨어요.

A Where did Ms. Kim go?

B She went to the library.

Grammar Points

A/V-(으)셨어요

'-(으)셨어요' is a combination of '-(으)시-' and the past tense sentence ending '-았어요/었어요'.

verb or adjective stems ending with a vowel + -셨어요 : 가다 → 가셨어요

verb or adjective stems ending with a consonant + -으셨어요 : 읽다 → 읽으셨어요

▶ Grammar Reference p.135

Practice

Complete each sentence using '-(으)셨어요'.

1) 어머니는 아침에 책을 ________________. (읽다)

2) 아버지는 어제 텔레비전을 ________________. (보다)

3) 할머니는 시장에 ________________. (가다)

4) 선생님은 코트를 ________________. (입다)

Answer 1) 읽으셨어요 2) 보셨어요 3) 가셨어요 4) 입으셨어요

Conversation Drills 대화 연습

Conversation

TRACK 03

A Jina, who is this?
B My father.
A What does he do for a living?
B He works at a bank.
A Who is this?
B My younger brother.
A What does he do?
B He is a student.

A 진아 씨, 이분은 누구세요?
B 우리 아버지세요.
A 아버지는 무슨 일을 하세요?
B 은행에서 일하세요.

A 이 사람은 누구예요?
B 제 동생이에요.
A 동생은 뭘 해요?
B 학생이에요.

Check it

1. 진아의 아버지는 은행원이에요.
   T F

2. 진아의 동생은 회사에 다녀요.
   T F

Answer 1. T 2. F

Practice the dialogue with your partner. Use the pictures below as cues.

Tasks & Activities 과제

Pair work

Part A

The following is the family tree of Junko. With your partner, ask and answer about Junko's family.

Pair work

Part B

The following is the family tree of Junko. With your partner, ask and answer about Junko's family.

Listening 듣기

TRACK 04

1. Listen to Yeongjun's talk and match each family member with their respective workplace.

1) 아버지

2) 어머니

3) 누나

4) 형

5) 동생

①  은행

②  백화점

③  병원

④  학교

⑤  회사

⑥  우체국

2. Write down Andy's sister's and brother's job.

앤디의 여동생

1) 직업 : ________

앤디의 남동생

2) 직업 : ________

TRACK 04

3. **Listen to the dialogue and choose the correct photo they are talking about.**

1)

① 

② 

③ 

2)

① 

② 

③ 

Answer **1.** 1) ⑤ 2) ③ 3) ② 4) ① 5) ④ **2.** 1) 회사원 2) 학생 **3.** 1) ① 2) ③

Reading & Writing 읽기와 쓰기

1. **Read the following descriptions and connect them with the corresponding family pictures.**

1)

우리 가족은 모두 다섯 명이에요. 아버지하고 어머니, 형이 한 명, 동생이 한 명 있어요. 아버지는 회사에 다니세요. 어머니는 은행원이세요. 형은 백화점에서 일해요. 동생은 대학생이에요.

①

2)

안녕하세요? 우리 가족은 모두 네 명이에요. 저하고 아내, 딸이 하나, 아들이 하나 있어요. 저는 우리 가족을 아주 사랑해요.

②

3)

우리 가족은 모두 네 명이에요. 남편하고 딸이 두 명 있어요. 우리 딸의 이름은 소라하고 소미예요. 소라는 지금 회사에 다녀요. 그리고 소미는 대학생이에요.

③

2. Attach a picture of your family and write a short passage introducing each family member.

Now I can...

- ☐ use honorific expressions
- ☐ introduce my family members
- ☐ talk about possessions

in Korean.

Answer 1. 1) ② 2) ③ 3) ①

Additional Expressions 추가 표현

Plain forms and honorific forms

There are some words that should be used to express respect towards a senior person.

Plain		Honorific	
이름	이름이 뭐예요? What is your name?	성함	성함이 어떻게 되세요? What is your name?
나이	나이가 몇 살이에요? How old are you?	연세	연세가 어떻게 되세요? How old are you?
생일	오늘은 친구 생일이에요. Today is my friend's birthday.	생신	오늘은 아버지 생신이에요. Today is my father's birthday.

With verbs, some take totally different basic forms to respect the subject of the verbs.

Plain		Honorific	
자다	아이가 자요. A baby is sleeping.	주무시다	할머니가 주무세요. My grandmother is sleeping.
먹다	동생이 점심을 먹어요. My younger sister/brother is eating lunch.	드시다	아버지가 점심을 드세요. My father is eating lunch.
있다	동생이 집에 있어요. My younger sister/brother is at home.	계시다	어머니가 집에 계세요. My mother is at home.
말하다	친구가 말해요. My friend is talking.	말씀하시다	선생님이 말씀하세요. The teacher is talking.
죽다	그 사람이 죽었어요. That person died.	돌아가시다	할아버지가 돌아가셨어요. My grandfather passed away.

UNIT 2

Transportation

교통

In This Unit

- Talking about transportation 교통수단 표현하기
- Talking about what one should do 당위 표현하기

Expressions 표현

인사동에 어떻게 가요?	Could you tell me how to get to Insa-dong?
걸어(서) 가요/와요.	I go/come on foot.
몇 번 버스를 타야 돼요?	What number bus should I take?
몇 호선을 타야 돼요?	Which subway line should I take?
여기에서 얼마나 걸려요?	How long does it take from here?

Vocabulary 어휘

Means of transportation

지하철 subway
배 ship / boat
비행기 airplane
택시 taxi
버스 bus
기차 train

Vocabulary related to transportation

타다 to get on / to ride
호선 subway line number
갈아타다 to transfer
번 counting unit after number
내리다 to get off

Subway stations

회현역 Hoehyeon Station
잠실역 Jamsil Station
동대문운동장역 Dongdaemun Stadium Station
서울대입구역 Seoul Nat'l Univ. Station
시청역 City Hall Station
사당역 Sadang Station
명동역 Myeongdong Station
남부터미널역 Nambu Bus Terminal Station
안국역 Anguk Station
고속터미널역 Express Bus Terminal Station
충무로역 Chungmuro Station
교대역 Seoul Nat'l Univ. of Education Station
을지로3가역 Euljiro 3-ga Station
삼성역 Samseong Station

Famous places

남대문시장 Namdaemun Market
경주 Gyeongju
코엑스몰 Coex Mall
예술의 전당 Seoul Arts Center
부산 Busan
인사동 Insa-dong
제주도 Jeju Island
명동 Myeong-dong
롯데월드 Lotte World

Question words

어떻게 how
얼마나 how long

Others

걷다 to walk
같이 together
수영 swimming
여자 woman / female
듣다 to listen / to hear

Key Dialogues 핵심 대화

Talking about transportation (1)

TRACK 05

A 뭘 타요?

B 지하철을 타요.

A What do you take?

B I take the subway.

> **Grammar Points**
>
> **N에서 N′을/를 타다**
>
> When expressing getting on a mode of transportation, the verb '타다' is used. '타다' requires an object and object particle '을/를'. After the place where one gets on, '에서' is attached.
>
> ▶ Grammar Reference p.135

A 남대문시장에 어떻게 가요?

B 학교 앞에서 버스를 타세요.

A Would you tell me how to get to Namdaemun Market?

B Take a bus in front of the school.

Practice

● With your partner, talk about how to get to the following destinations.

남대문시장에 어떻게 가요?

버스를 타세요.

남대문시장

버스

제주도

배

명동

지하철

경주

기차

부산

비행기

Talking about transportation (2)

TRACK 05

Grammar Points

N에서 내리다

When expressing getting off at a place, 'N에서 내리다' is used.

▶ Grammar Reference p.135

A 어디에서 내려요?

B 회현역에서 내리세요.

A Where should I get off?

B Get off at Hoehyeon Station.

Practice

With your partner, talk about where you should get off.

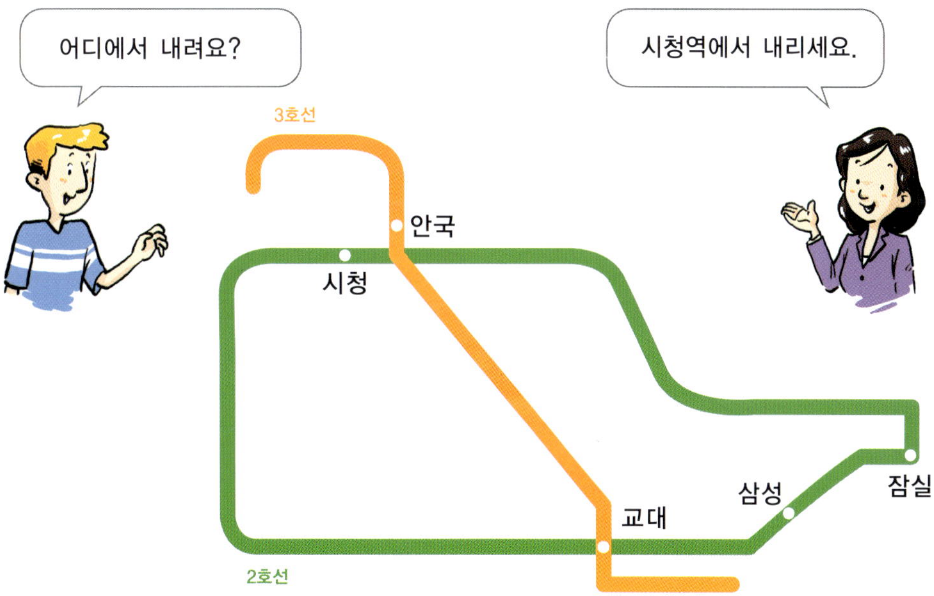

Talking about transportation (3)

TRACK 05

Grammar Points

N에서 N'(으)로 갈아타다

When expressing transferring, the verb '갈아타다' is used. '(으)로' comes after the mode of transportation one transfer to. '에서' follows the place where one transfers.

▶ Grammar Reference p.135

A 어디에서 갈아타요?

B 교대역에서 삼 호선으로 갈아타세요.

A Where should I transfer?

B Transfer to line 3 at Seoul Nat'l Univ. of Education Station.

Practice

● With your partner, talk about where you should transfer.

어디에서 갈아타요?

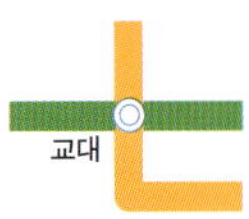

교대역, 3호선

교대역에서 삼 호선으로 갈아타세요.

사당역, 4호선

시청역, 1호선

잠실역, 8호선

고속터미널역, 7호선

Talking about how to get to somewhere

TRACK 05

A 집에 어떻게 가요?

B 버스를 타고 가요.

A How do you go home?

B I go by bus.

A 학교에 어떻게 와요?

B 걸어서 와요.

A How do you come to school?

B I come (to school) on foot.

Grammar Points

N을/를 타고 가다/오다

'타고 가다/오다' is used to show by what mode of transportation one goes/comes to a place. To simply express what mode of transportation is taken, use the verb '타다'. When expressing 'come/go on foot', the pattern '걸어(서) 가다/오다' is used.

▶ Grammar Reference p.135

Practice

1 Ask your partner how to get to the following destinations.

집에 어떻게 가요?

집 / 

버스를 타고 가요.

코엑스몰 백화점 학교 부산

2 Change the verbs below into the right form.

1) 걷다 + -어요 → ________

2) 듣다 + -었어요 → ________

3) 걷다 + -으세요 → ________

4) 듣다 + -지만 → ________

Grammar Points

'ㄷ' irregular verbs

'ㄷ' in 'ㄷ' irregular verbs such as '걷다', '듣다' changes into 'ㄹ', when combined with the ending beginning with vowels as in '걸어요' and '들어요'.

▶ Grammar Reference p.136

Answer 2 1) 걸어요 2) 들었어요 3) 걸으세요 4) 들지만

Talking about what one should do

TRACK 05

A 몇 번 버스를 타야 돼요?

B 오 번 버스를 타야 돼요.

A What number bus should I take?

B You should take number 5.

A 오늘 뭐 해요?

B 책을 읽어야 돼요.

A What are you doing today?

B I should read a book.

Grammar Points

V-아야/어야 되다

'-아야/어야 되다' means 'should', 'ought to' or 'must'.

verb stem's last vowels ending with 'ㅏ' or 'ㅗ' + -아야 돼요 : 가다 → 가야 돼요

verbs ending with '하다', 하다 → 해야 돼요 : 공부하다 → 공부해야 돼요

In all other cases, add '-어야 돼요' : 읽다 → 읽어야 돼요

▶ Grammar Reference p.136

Notes

Subway lines are expressed as '일 호선, 이 호선, 삼 호선,…' and the Korean expression for 'which subway line' is '몇 호선'. Bus numbers are expressed as '일 번, 이 번, 삼 번,…' and the Korean expression for 'what number' is '몇 번'.

Practice

Change the following verbs into '-아야/어야 돼요' pattern.

가다 → 가야 돼요

1) 타다 → ____________ 2) 오다 → ____________

3) 내리다 → ____________ 4) 운동하다 → ____________

Answer 1) 타야 돼요 2) 와야 돼요 3) 내려야 돼요 4) 운동해야 돼요

Conversation Drills 대화 연습

Conversation 1

TRACK 06

A Would you tell me how to get to Namdaemun Market?

B Take the subway.

A What line should I take?

B Take line number 2. And transfer to line 4 at Sadang Station.

A 남대문시장에 어떻게 가요?

B 지하철을 타세요.

A 몇 호선을 타야 돼요?

B 이 호선을 타세요. 그리고 사당역에서 사 호선으로 갈아타세요.

Check it

1. 남대문시장에 가요. T F
2. 버스를 타야 돼요. T F
3. 1호선을 타요. T F

Answer 1. T 2. F 3. F

Role-play the dialogue with your partner. Use the subway map below as cues. You are at the Namdaemun Market.

Conversation 2

TRACK 06

A Where should I get off?
B You should get off at Hoehyeon Station.
A How long does it take from here?
B It takes about 40 minutes.

A 어디에서 내려야 돼요?
B 회현역에서 내려야 돼요.
A 여기에서 얼마나 걸려요?
B 사십 분쯤 걸려요.

Check it

1. 회현역에서 지하철을 탔어요.
   T F

2. 회현역까지 40분쯤 걸려요.
   T F

Answer 1. F 2. T

Role-play the dialogue with your partner.

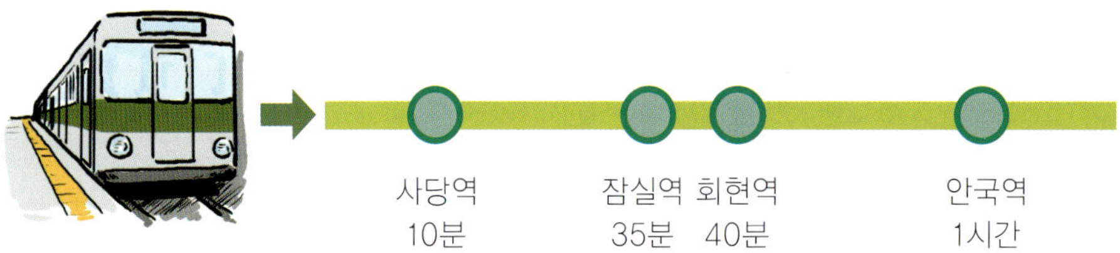

Tasks & Activities 과제

Group Work

You are inviting friends over to your house. Tell your friends how to get to your house.

애니 씨 집

3번 버스

Where to take a bus(subway): 학교 앞

Where to get off: 서울백화점 앞

How long it takes: 30분

________ 씨 집

____

Where to take a bus(subway): __________

Where to get off: __________

How long it takes: __________

________ 씨 집

____

Where to take a bus(subway): __________

Where to get off: __________

How long it takes: __________

________ 씨 집

____

Where to take a bus(subway): __________

Where to get off: __________

How long it takes: __________

Listening 듣기

TRACK 07

1. **Listen carefully and match each place with the correct subway station.**

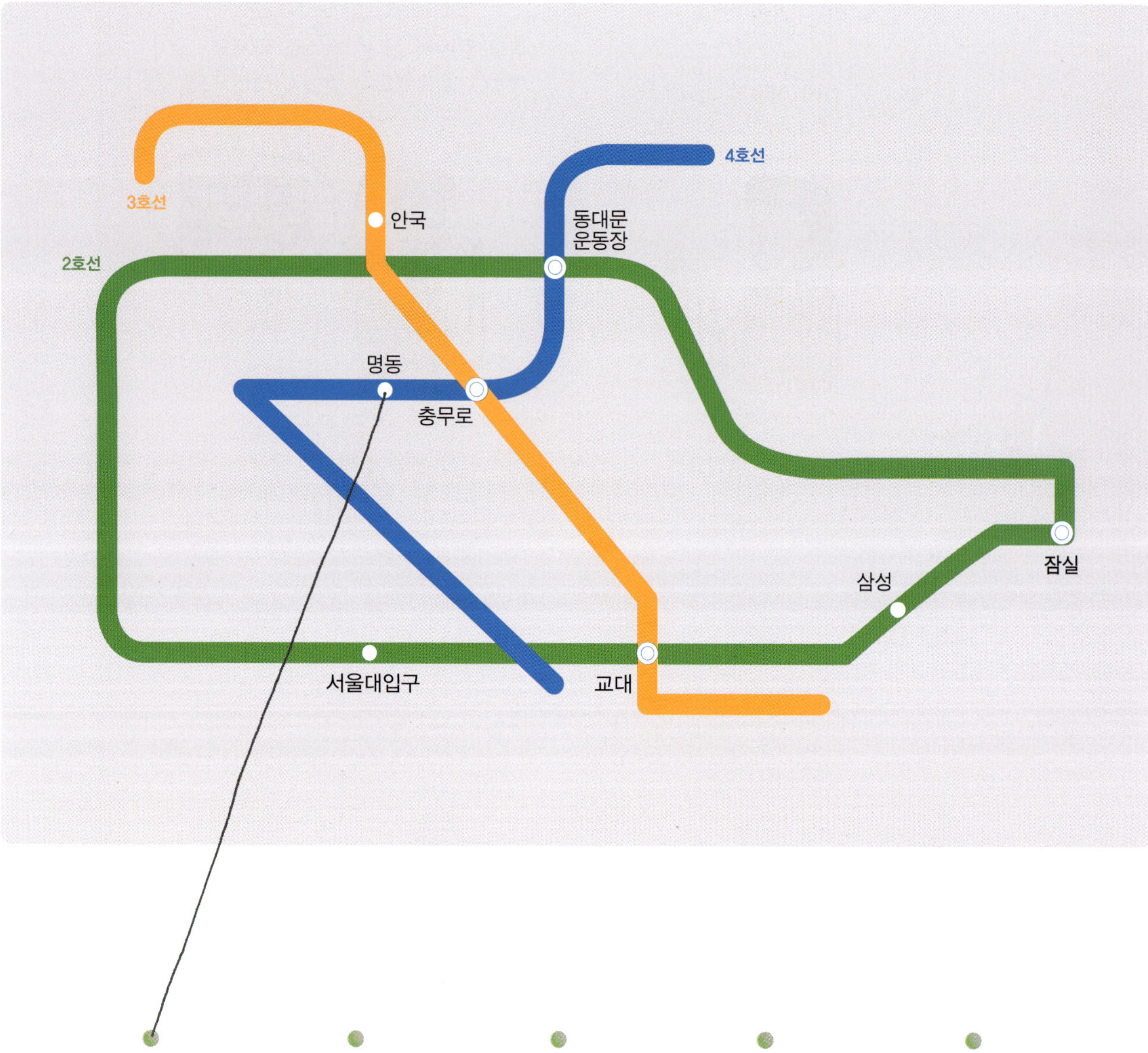

1) 명동 2) 애니 씨 집 3) 한국대학교 4) 서울시장 5) 하나극장

2. What should he do? Match each name with the correct picture.

1) 마이클 ●

① 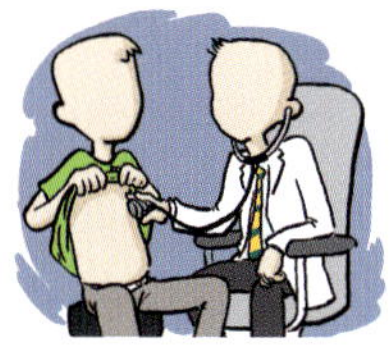

② 

2) 영준 ●

③ 

3) 앤디 ●

④ 

4) 토니 ●

⑤ 

3. Listen carefully and match.

1) 병원 ●	● 택시 ●	● 1시간
2) 시장 ●	● 버스 ●	● 30분
3) 백화점 ●	● 지하철 ●	● 10분
	● 걸어서 ●	

Answer **1.** 1) 명동 2) 잠실 3) 안국 4) 동대문운동장 5) 삼성 **2.** 1) ④ 2) ① 3) ⑤ 4) ③ **3.** 1) 병원 – 지하철 – 30분 2) 시장 – 택시 – 10분 3) 백화점 – 버스 – 1시간

Reading & Writing 읽기와 쓰기

1. Read and answer the questions.

나는 오늘 병원에 가요. 집 앞에서 버스를 타요. 그리고 학교 앞에서 내려요. 집에서 학교 앞까지 한 시간쯤 걸려요. 학교 앞에서 병원까지 걸어서 가요. 십 분쯤 걸려요.

1) 집에서 병원까지 어떻게 가요?

① 

② 

③ 

2) 집에서 병원까지 얼마나 걸려요? _____시간 _____분

2. Using the passage above as a model, write down where you are going today, how you are going there, and how long it takes.

나는 오늘 ________에 가요. ______________________________

____

____

____

____

____

Now I can...

- ☐ talk about transportation
- ☐ talk about what one should do

in Korean.

Answer 1. 1) ③ 2) 1, 10

Additional Expressions 추가 표현

In a taxi

학교 앞에서 세워 주세요 / 내려 주세요.
Please stop in front of the school.

똑바로 가 주세요.
Go straight, please.

좌회전해 주세요.
Turn left, please.

우회전해 주세요.
Turn right, please.

Types of trains in Korea

고속전철(KTX)

The fastest train in Korea put into service in 2004. Runs as fast as 300km/h.

새마을호

The second fastest train in Korea

무궁화호

A train with service one level lower than Saemaeul

UNIT 3

Reason

이유

In This Unit

- Talking about what one cannot do 하지 못하는 것 말하기
- Giving reasons 이유 표현하기
- Declining 거절하기

Expressions 표현

미안하지만 일요일에는 약속이 있어요.
I'm sorry but I have an appointment on Sunday.

약속이 있어서 안 돼요.
I can't because I have an appointment.

Vocabulary 어휘

Nouns

중국어 Chinese (language)
자전거 bicycle
프랑스어 French (language)
요리 cooking
피아노 piano
기타 guitar
운전 driving

테니스 tennis
스키 skiing
표 ticket
휴가 leave / vacation
외국 foreign country
세일 sale
약속 appointment

일 work
숙제 homework
축구 soccer
청소 cleaning
공항 airport
수영장 swimming pool
남자 man/male

뉴스 news
드라마 drama (TV series)
설렁탕 Seolleongtang

Verbs

끝내다 to finish
치다 to play / to hit / to strike
찍다 to take (a picture)
들다 to be contained

Adjectives

맵다 hot / spicy
피곤하다 tired
작다 small

춥다 cold
덥다 hot
어렵다 difficult

시끄럽다 noisy
미안하다 sorry

많다 many / much
쉽다 easy

Others

왜 why
많이 many / much

이번 this time

너무 too

-들 plural marker

Words that go together

중국어를 하다 to speak Chinese
피아노를 치다 to play the piano

테니스를 치다 to play tennis
스키를 타다 to ski
일이 많다 to have a lot of work to do

시험이 있다 to have a test

사진을 찍다 to take a picture

Key Dialogues 핵심 대화

Talking about what one cannot or could not do

TRACK 08

A 중국어 해요?

B 아니요, 못해요.

A Can you speak Chinese?

B No, I can't.

> **Grammar Points**
>
> 못 V
>
> '못' followed by a verb means that one doesn't have the ability to do something or something is simply not possible.
>
> ▶▶ Grammar Reference p.136

A 어제 학교에 갔어요?

B 아니요, 못 갔어요.

A Did you go to school yesterday?

B No, I couldn't go.

Practice

Ask your partner whether he/she is able to do the following and check(✓) on what he/she is able to do.

자전거를 타요?
네, 자전거를 타요.

중국어를 해요?
아니요, 중국어를 못해요.

 □ 자전거를 타다

□ 중국어를 하다

□ 영어를 하다

□ 프랑스어를 하다

 □ 요리를 하다
 □ 피아노를 치다
 □ 기타를 치다
 □ 운전을 하다

 □ 테니스를 치다
 □ 수영을 하다
 □ 태권도를 하다
 □ 스키를 타다

Giving a reason (1)

TRACK 08

A 왜 영화를 못 봤어요?

B 표가 없어서 못 봤어요.

A Why couldn't you watch the movie?

B I couldn't because there were no tickets.

A 왜 김치를 못 먹어요?

B 매워서 못 먹어요.

A Why can't you eat kimchi?

B I can't because it is spicy.

Notes

When asking for a reason, '왜', which means 'why', is used.

Grammar Points

A/V-아서/어서

'-아서/어서' means 'because/since/so'. It is used to connect two clauses. The first clause contains the reason for the following clause.

verb or adjective stem's last vowels ending with 'ㅏ' or 'ㅗ' + -아서 : 비싸다 → 비싸서

verbs or adjectives ending with '하다', 하다 → 해서 : 복잡하다 → 복잡해서

In all other cases, add '-어서' : 있다 → 있어서

▶ Grammar Reference p.136

Practice

1 Look at the pictures and complete each sentence.

1)  피곤하다

_________ 책을 못 읽어요.

2)  비싸다

구두가 _________ 안 샀어요.

3)  작다

옷이 _________ 못 입어요.

4)  복잡하다

길이 _________ 지하철을 타요.

2 Change the words below as shown in the example.

맵다 → 매워서

1) 춥다 → _____________ 2) 덥다 → _____________

3) 어렵다 → _____________ 4) 시끄럽다 → _____________

Grammar Points

'ㅂ' irregular adjectives

When adjectives whose stems end with 'ㅂ' meet the ending which begins with a vowel as '아/어' or '으', 'ㅂ' changes into '우'.

맵다 : 맵 + -어요 → 매워요

맵 + -어서 → 매워서

▶ Grammar Reference p.137

Answer **1** 1) 피곤해서 2) 비싸서 3) 작아서 4) 복잡해서 **2** 1) 추워서 2) 더워서 3) 어려워서 4) 시끄러워서

Giving a reason (2)

TRACK 08

A 왜 케이크를 샀어요?

B 친구 생일이라서 케이크를 샀어요.

A Why did you buy the cake?

B I bought it because it is my friend's birthday.

Grammar Points

N(이)라서

Together with a noun, this pattern shows the reason for the sentence that follows.

휴가예요. + 회사에 안 가요.

→ 휴가라서 회사에 안 가요.

nouns ending with a vowel + -라서 : 휴가 → 휴가라서

nouns ending with a consonant + -이라서 : 외국 사람 → 외국 사람이라서

▶ Grammar Reference p.137

Practice

Complete the sentences below using the words in the box.

생일이라서	월요일이라서
세일이라서	한국 사람이라서
휴가라서	

1) ______________ 회사에 안 가요.
2) ______________ 파티를 해요.
3) ______________ 백화점에 사람이 많이 있어요.
4) ______________ 김치를 좋아해요.

Giving two or more alternatives

TRACK 08

A 이번 일요일에 같이 영화 볼까요?

B 미안하지만 일요일에는 약속이 있어요.
금요일이나 토요일은 어때요?

A 그럼 금요일에 봐요.

A Shall we watch a movie together this Sunday?

B I am sorry but I have an appointment on Sunday.
How about Friday or Saturday?

A Then, let's watch it on Friday.

Grammar Points

N(이)나 N′

When suggesting two alternative nouns, '(이)나' is added to the first of the two choices to connect the two nouns.

nouns ending with a vowel + 나 : 버스 → 버스나

nouns ending with a consonant + 이나 : 토요일 → 토요일이나

▶ Grammar Reference p.138

Notes

When turning down an offer politely, it is better to say '미안하지만', which means 'I'm sorry but', in advance.

Practice

Complete the sentences using '(이)나'.

1)  
콜라 주스
______________________ 를 주세요.

2)  
신문 책
______________________ 을 읽어요.

3)  
버스 지하철
______________________ 을 타고 가요.

4) 

5월 3일 5월 4일
______________________ 에 만날까요?

Answer 1) 콜라나 주스 2) 신문이나 책 3) 버스나 지하철 4) 5월 3일이나 5월 4일

Conversation Drills 대화 연습

Conversation 1 TRACK 09

A Annie, have you finished the work?
B No, I haven't.
A Why not?
B Because I didn't have enough time.

A 애니 씨, 일을 끝냈어요?
B 아니요, 못 끝냈어요.
A 왜 못 끝냈어요?
B 시간이 없어서 못 끝냈어요.

Check it

애니 씨는 일을 못 끝냈어요.

T F

Answer: T

Practice the dialogue with your partner using the sentences provided in the box.

Something one couldn't do	Reason
일을 끝내다	시간이 없다
주말에 쉬다	숙제가 많다
친구를 만나다	일이 많다
영화를 보다	표가 없다
생일 파티에 가다	피곤하다

Conversation 2

TRACK 09

A Wei, shall we watch a movie together this Saturday?

B I can't because I have an appointment on Saturday.

A How about Sunday then?

B I'm sorry but I have to work on Sunday.

A Then, shall we watch it on Thursday or Friday?

B Ok, let's watch it on Friday.

A 웨이 씨, 이번 토요일에 같이 영화 볼까요?

B 토요일에는 약속이 있어서 안 돼요.

A 일요일은 어때요?

B 미안하지만 일요일에는 일을 해야 돼요.

A 그럼 목요일이나 금요일에 볼까요?

B 좋아요. 금요일에 봐요.

Check it

1. 웨이는 토요일에 약속이 있어요. [T] [F]

2. 두 사람은 일요일에 영화를 봐요. [T] [F]

Answer 1. [T] 2. [F]

Practice the dialogue with your partner. Use the information below as cues.

A
영화 보다
테니스 치다
공원에 가다
축구를 하다
산에 가다

B: 토요일	B: 일요일
약속이 있다	일을 해야 되다
약속이 있다	도서관에 가야 되다
일이 있다	공부해야 되다
일이 많다	청소를 해야 되다
시간이 없다	숙제를 해야 되다

Tasks & Activities 과제

Group Work

Form two groups. Make as many sentences as possible choosing the best reason from the "Reason" linking with a sentence from the "What one can't". The group that makes more sentences wins.

Reason	What one can't
돈이 없어요.	수영을 못 해요.
시간이 없어요.	운동을 못 해요.
카메라가 없어요.	친구를 못 만나요.
피곤해요.	카메라를 못 사요.
어려워요.	운전을 못 해요.
비행기 표가 없어요.	파티에 못 가요.
술을 마셨어요.	미국에 못 가요.
매워요.	이 책을 못 읽어요.
내일 시험이 있어요.	이 음식을 못 먹어요.
더워요.	택시를 못 타요.
추워요.	걸어서 못 가요.
길이 복잡해요.	사진을 못 찍어요.

Listening 듣기

TRACK 10

1. Listen carefully and connect each person with the correct picture expressing the reason why the person couldn't go.

1) 
영준

2) 
라주

3) 
크리스

① 

② 

③ 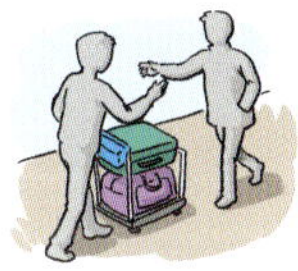

④ 

2. Listen to the dialogue and choose the correct answer.

1) ① 시간이 없어서　② 표가 없어서　③ 일이 있어서
2) ① 금요일　② 토요일　③ 일요일

3. Listen to the dialogue and mark O for True, and mark X for False.

1) 남자는 고기를 좋아해요. (　　)
2) 불고기가 비싸서 비빔밥을 먹어요. (　　)

Answer 1. 1) ③ 2) ② 3) ①
2. 1) ② 2) ③ 3. 1) X 2) X

Reading & Writing 읽기와 쓰기

1. Read the following passage and number the pictures to show the order in which things happened.

오늘은 일요일이라서 9시쯤 일어났어요. 우유를 마시고 텔레비전을 봤어요. 뉴스는 너무 어려워서 드라마를 봤어요. 재미있어서 두 시간쯤 봤어요. 12시쯤 식당에 갔어요. 사람이 많아서 30분쯤 기다려야 됐어요. 저는 날씨가 추워서 설렁탕을 먹었어요.

① 

② 

③ 

④ 

⑤ 

④ → ____ → ____ → ____ → ____

2. Look at the pictures and complete the story.

오늘 나는 여덟 시 삼십 분에 일어났어요.

____

____

____

Now I can...

- ☐ talk about what I can't do
- ☐ give a reason
- ☐ decline

in Korean.

Answer 1. ④ → ③ → ② → ⑤ → ①

Additional Expressions 추가 표현

When apologizing

밤늦게 전화해서 죄송합니다.
I'm sorry to call you so late at night.

늦어서 미안해요.
I am sorry that I am late.

늦어서 죄송합니다.
I am sorry that I am late. (more polite)

연락이 늦어서 죄송합니다.
I'm sorry to be contacting you so late.

약속을 못 지켜서 죄송합니다.
I'm sorry that I couldn't keep my promise/our appointment.

When showing gratitude

와 주셔서 감사합니다.
Thank you for coming.

도와줘서 고마워요.
Thank you for your help.

도와주셔서 감사합니다.
Thank you for your help. (more polite)

전화해 주셔서 감사합니다.
Thank you for calling.

초대해 주셔서 감사합니다.
Thank you for inviting me.

UNIT 4

Post Office
우체국

In This Unit

- Talking about future plans 미래 표현하기
- Talking about means or methods 도구, 수단 표현하기
- Talking about conditions 조건 표현하기

Expressions 표 현

안에 뭐가 들었어요?	What's inside? / What's in it?
책이 들었어요.	There is a book inside.
미국까지 얼마나 걸려요?	How long does it take to get to the U.S.?
한 달쯤 걸려요.	It takes about a month.

Vocabulary 어 휘

Vocabulary related to the post office

보내다 to send / to mall
편지 lcttcr
엽서 postcard
소포 parcel
부치다 to send / to mail

Continents & Countries

베트남 Vietnam
유럽 Europe
아프리카 Africa
말레이시아 Malaysia
브라질 Brasil

Term / Period

일 day
주일 week
달 month

Others

숟가락 spoon
비 rain
괜찮다 alright
젓가락 chopsticks
눈 snow
여행 trip / travel
포크 fork
눈사람 snowman
한복 hanbok (traditional Korean costume)
손 hand
나쁘다 bad
끝나다 to be finished
배고프다 hungry

Words that go together

비가 오다 to rain
눈이 오다 to snow
여행을 가다 to take a trip / to go on a trip

Key Dialogues 핵심 대화

Talking about future plans

TRACK 11

A 어디로 보내실 거예요?

B 캐나다로 보낼 거예요.

A Where are you going to send it?

B I am going to send it to Canada.

Grammar Points

V-(으)ㄹ 거예요

'-(으)ㄹ 거예요' indicates the subject's future plans or intentions.

verb stems ending with a vowel + -ㄹ 거예요 : 가다 → 갈 거예요

verb stems ending with a consonant + -을 거예요 : 읽다 → 읽을 거예요

▶ Grammar Reference p.138

Practice

Change the endings of the verbs below using '-(으)ㄹ 거예요'.

가다 → 갈 거예요

1) 자다 → ________________

2) 보다 → ________________

3) 먹다 → ________________

4) 입다 → ________________

Answer 1) 잘 거예요 2) 볼 거예요 3) 먹을 거예요 4) 입을 거예요

Talking about means or methods

TRACK 11

Grammar Points

N(으)로

'(으)로' indicates the means or method.

nouns ending with a vowel + 로
: 비행기 → 비행기로

nouns ending with a consonant + 으로 : 젓가락 → 젓가락으로

For nouns with 'ㄹ' ending, only '로' is added.
지하철 → 지하철로
연필 → 연필로

▶ Grammar Reference p.138

A 뭐로 보내실 거예요?
B 비행기로 보내 주세요.

A How would you like to send this?
B By airmail, please.

Practice

With your partner, talk about what you can do with the following items.

Telling what's inside

TRACK 11

A 안에 뭐가 들었어요?

B 책이 들었어요.

A What's inside?

B There are books inside.

Notes

When asking and telling the contents inside, the pattern 'N이/가 들었어요' is used.

책이 들었어요.

Practice

Ask and answer about what's inside of each box.

안에 뭐가 들었어요?

시계가 들었어요.

1)

______________.

2)

______________.

3)

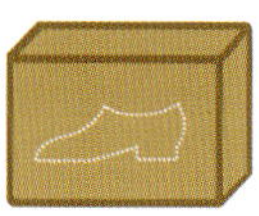

______________.

4)

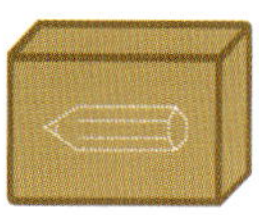

______________.

Answer 1) 우산이 들었어요 2) 모자가 들었어요 3) 구두가 들었어요 4) 연필이 들었어요

Talking about conditions

TRACK 11

Grammar Points

A/V-(으)면

'-(으)면' indicates conditions or assumptions.

verb or adjective stems ending with a vowel + -면 : 끝나다 → 끝나면

verb or adjective stems ending with a consonant + -으면 : 있다 → 있으면

▶▶ Grammar Reference p.139

A 비행기로 보내면 얼마나 걸려요?

B 비행기로 보내면 일주일쯤 걸려요.

A How long does it take if I send by plane?

B It takes about a week if you send by plane.

Notes

When counting days and weeks, '일, 이, 삼, 사,···' is used.

3일 → 삼 일
3주일 → 삼 주일

When counting months, '한, 두, 세, 네,···' is used.

3달 → 세 달

Practice

Write down what you would do in the weathers below as shown in the example.

날씨가 좋아요.	-	산에 가요.	⇨ 날씨가 좋으면 산에 가요.
1) 비가 와요.	-	집에서 공부해요.	⇨ ______________________.
2) 날씨가 추워요.	-	커피를 마셔요.	⇨ ______________________.
3) 눈이 와요.	-	눈사람을 만들어요.	⇨ ______________________.
4) 날씨가 나빠요.	-	집에서 쉬어요.	⇨ ______________________.

Answer 1) 비가 오면 집에서 공부해요. 2) 날씨가 추우면 커피를 마셔요. 3) 눈이 오면 눈사람을 만들어요. 4) 날씨가 나쁘면 집에서 쉬어요.

Indicating the receiver

TRACK 11

Grammar Points

N한테

Adding '한테' to a person, denotes that he/she is the receiver of the action described.

▶ Grammar Reference p.139

A 누구한테 이 소포를 보낼 거예요?

B 동생한테 보낼 거예요.

A To whom are you going to send this parcel?

B I am going to send it to my brother.

Practice

Look at the pictures and complete the sentences as shown in the example.

 →  친구 ⇨ 친구한테 꽃을 줘요.

1)  →  동생 ⇨ ______________ 줘요.

2)  →  언니 ⇨ ______________ 부쳐요.

3)  →  딸 ⇨ ______________ 줘요.

4)  →  형 ⇨ ______________ 보내요.

Answer 1) 동생한테 사과를 2) 언니한테 소포를 3) 딸한테 아이스크림을 4) 형한테 편지를

Conversation Drills 대화 연습

Conversation

TRACK 12

A 어디로 보내실 거예요?

B 미국으로 보낼 거예요.

A 안에 뭐가 들었어요?

B 책하고 옷이 들었어요.

미국까지 얼마나 걸려요?

A 비행기로 보내면 일주일쯤 걸려요. 그리고 배로 보내면 한 달쯤 걸려요.

B 그럼 비행기로 보내 주세요. 얼마예요?

A 이만 팔천 원이에요.

B 여기 있어요.

A Where are you going to send it?

B I am going to send it to the U.S.

A What's inside?

B Books and clothes. How long does it take to the U.S.?

A It takes about a week if you send by plane. And it takes about a month if you send by ship.

B Then I'll send it by plane. How much is it?

A It is 28,000 won.

B Here it is.

Check it

1. 미국으로 소포를 보내고 있어요. T F

2. 배로 소포를 보낼 거예요. T F

Answer 1. T 2. F

Practice the dialogue with your partner. Use the information below as cues.

비행기				배			
일본 중국	인도 베트남 말레이시아	미국 유럽 호주	브라질 아프리카	일본 중국	인도 베트남 말레이시아	미국 유럽 호주	브라질 아프리카
19,000원	22,000원	28,000원	34,000원	10,000원	12,000원	15,000원	18,000원
5일		1주일		3주일		한 달	

 책

 옷

 CD

 가방

 사전

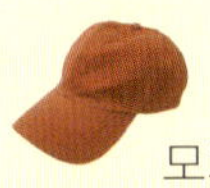 모자

Tasks & Activities 과제

Group Work

Write down what you would do in the following situations and then ask your classmates what he/she would do.

질문 / 이름	애니		
배고프면	빵을 먹어요.		
더우면	샤워를 해요.		
추우면	코트를 입어요.		
비가 오면	집에서 쉬어요.		
돈이 없으면	밥을 안 먹어요.		
시간이 없으면	택시를 타요.		

Listening 듣기

TRACK 13

1. **Listen carefully and connect the pictures on the left with corresponding pictures on the right.**

1) 

2) 

3) 

4) 

① 

② 

③ 

④ 

⑤ 

2. **Listen carefully and choose the correct answer.**

1) ① 미국 ② 인도 ③ 중국

2) ____________

3. **Listen carefully and choose the correct answer.**

1) ①  ②  ③ 

2) ① 친구 ② 동생 ③ 어머니

Answer 1. 1) ③ 2) ④ 3) ② 4) ⑤ 2. 1) ③ 2) 비행기 3. 1) ① 2) ②

Reading & Writing 읽기와 쓰기

1. **Read the postcard and mark O for True, and mark X for False.**

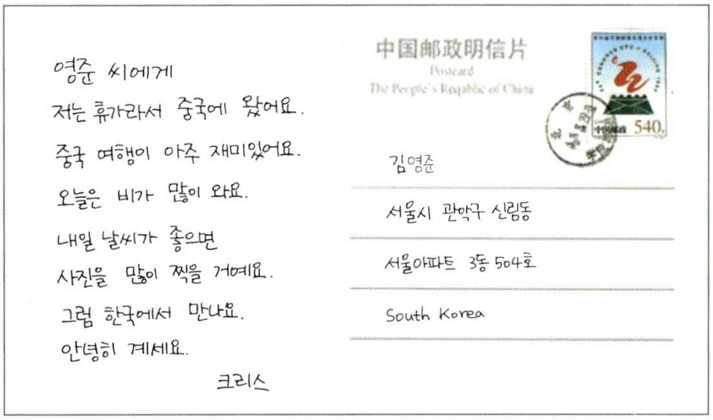

1) 크리스 씨는 친구한테 엽서를 보냈어요. ( )
2) 오늘은 날씨가 아주 좋아요. ( )
3) 크리스 씨는 한국에 갈 거예요. ( )

2. **Imagine you are on a trip, and write a postcard to your friend.**

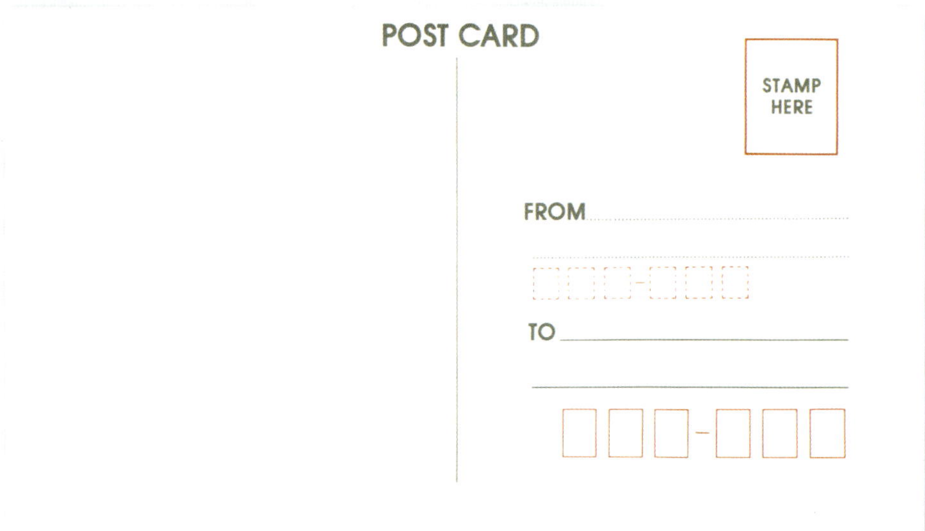

Now I can...

- ☐ talk about future plans
- ☐ talk about conditions
- ☐ send a postcard or a parcel at the post office

in Korean.

Answer 1. 1) O 2) X 3) O

Additional Expressions 추가 표현

How to write the address on an envelope

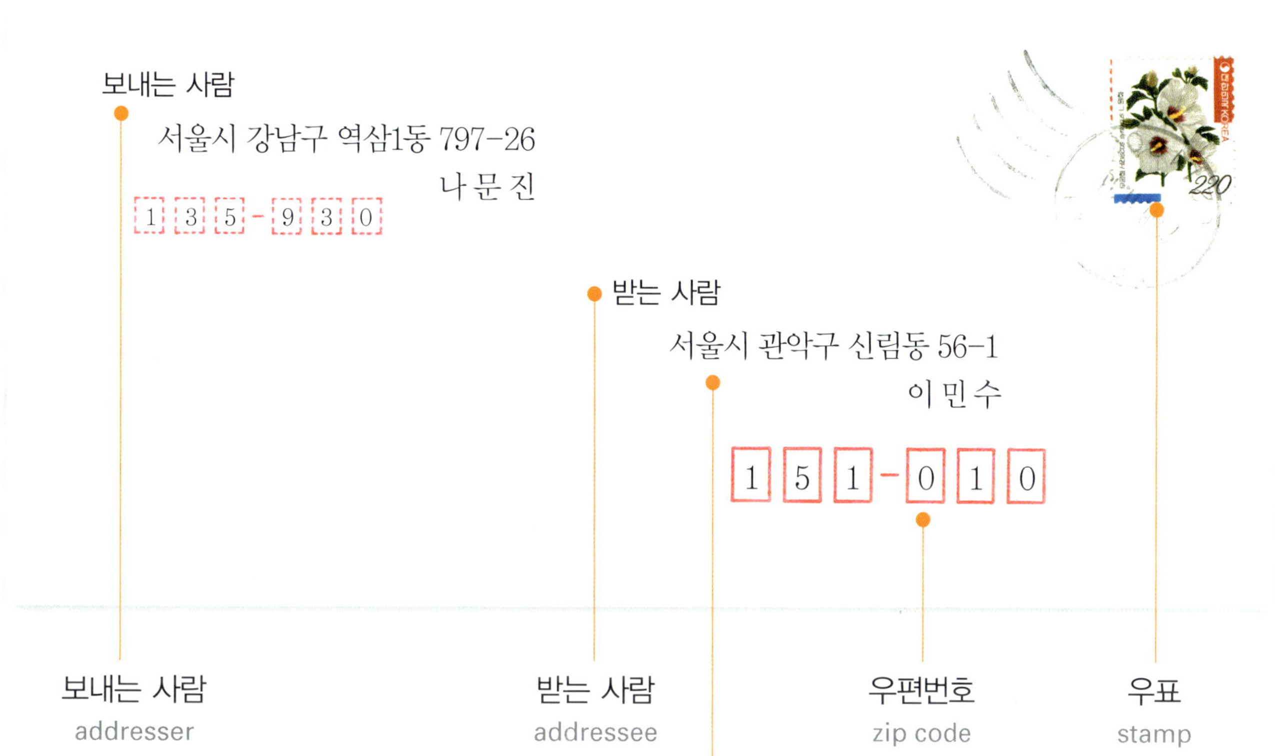

In Korea, you should write the address in order of district size, from the large district to smaller district, on an envelope.

Another way to count days

일 일	이 일	삼 일	사 일	오 일	십 일	십오 일
하루	**이틀**	**사흘**	**나흘**	**닷새**	**열흘**	**보름**
one day	two days	three days	four days	five days	ten days	fifteen days

UNIT 5

Reservations

예약

In This Unit

- Making reservations 예약하기
- Talking about hopes 희망 표현하기
- Talking about possibility and ability 가능, 능력 표현하기

Expressions 표현

열 시 비행기에 자리 있어요?	Is there any vacant seat on the 10 o'clock plane?
얼마 동안 계실 거예요?	How long are you going to stay?
요금이 어떻게 돼요?	Could you tell me how much the fare is?
성함이 어떻게 되세요?	May I have your name?

Vocabulary 어휘

Vocabulary related to reservations

예약하다 to reserve
자리 seat / place
기차표 train ticket
계시다 to be / to stay (honorific)
요금 fare / charge
전화번호 telephone number
출발하다 to depart
침대 방 room with a bed
온돌방 traditional Korean room / hot-floored room
성함 name (honorific)
출발 departure
도착하다 to arrive

Name of cities

런던 London
뉴욕 New York
도쿄 Tokyo
방콕 Bangkok
파리 Paris
로마 Rome
베이징 Beijing
마드리드 Madrid

Verbs

여행하다 to travel
운전하다 to drive
투표하다 to vote
피우다 to smoke (a cigarette)

Adjectives

바쁘다 busy
재미없다 not interesting

Nouns

바다 sea / ocean
음악 music
방학 school holidays
하루 one day
공 zero
손님 customer / guest
직원 staff
살 -years old/counting unit for age
결혼 marriage
투표 vote
인천공항 Incheon Airport
시내 downtown
이메일 e-mail
년 year

Words that go together

담배를 피우다 to smoke a cigarette

Key Dialogues 핵심 대화

Talking about possibility or ability

TRACK 14

A 지금 비행기 표 예약할 수 있어요?

B 네, 하실 수 있어요.

A Can I book a plane ticket?

B Yes, you can.

> **Grammar Points**
>
> **V-(으)ㄹ 수 있다**
>
> '-(으)ㄹ 수 있다' is used to express possibility or ability.
>
> verb stems ending with a vowel + -ㄹ 수 있어요
> : 치다 → 칠 수 있어요
>
> verb stems ending with a consonant + -을 수 있어요
> : 먹다 → 먹을 수 있어요
>
> ▶ Grammar Reference p.139

A 테니스를 칠 수 있어요?

B 아니요, 못 쳐요.

A Can you play tennis?

B No, I can't.

Practice

Change the following into '-(으)ㄹ 수 있어요' pattern.

피아노를 칠 수 있어요. (피아노를 치다)

1) ______________________. (같이 가다)

2) ______________________. (내일 만나다)

3) ______________________. (한국어 책을 읽다)

4) ______________________. (바다에서 수영하다)

Answer 1) 같이 갈 수 있어요 2) 내일 만날 수 있어요 3) 한국어 책을 읽을 수 있어요 4) 바다에서 수영할 수 있어요

Buying tickets

TRACK 14

A 열 시 비행기에 자리 있어요?

B 네, 있는데요.

A Is there any vacant seat on the 10 o'clock plane?

B Yes, there is.

A 일곱 시 기차표가 없는데요.

B 그럼 여덟 시 표는 있어요?

A There is no ticket for the 7 o'clock train.

B Then, are there tickets for the 8 o'clock train?

Grammar Points

A-(으)ㄴ데요/V-는데요

'-(으)ㄴ데요/는데요' is the sentence ending often used in spoken language. And it sounds more polite than '-아요/어요'.

'-(으)ㄴ데요' is attached to adjectives while '-는데요' is used for verbs.

verb stems + -는데요 : 먹다 → 먹는데요

adjective stems ending with a vowel + -ㄴ데요 : 바쁘다 → 바쁜데요

adjective stems ending with a consonant + -은데요 : 작다 → 작은데요

For adjectives ending in '있다' or '없다', '-는데요' is added, even though they are not verbs.

▶ Grammar Reference p.139

Practice

Change the words below as shown in the example.

가다 → 가는데요

1) 먹다 → ________ 2) 비싸다 → ________

3) 읽다 → ________ 4) 보다 → ________

5) 재미있다 → ________ 6) 춥다 → ________

Answer 1) 먹는데요 2) 비싼데요 3) 읽는데요 4) 보는데요 5) 재미있는데요 6) 추운데요

When expressing what one wants to do

TRACK 14

A 비행기 표를 예약하고 싶은데요.

B 어디로 가실 거예요?

A 런던으로 갈 거예요.

A I'd like to reserve a plane ticket.

B Where are you going?

A I am going to London.

> **Grammar Points**
>
> **V-고 싶다**
>
> '-고 싶다' is used to express the subject's hope.
>
> 가다 → 가고 싶어요
>
> ▶ Grammar Reference p.140

A 무슨 영화를 보고 싶어요?

B '친구'를 보고 싶어요.

A What movie do you want to see?

B I'd like to see 'Friends'.

Practice

With your partner talk about what you want to do using '-고 싶어요' and the pictures provided below.

뭘 하고 싶어요?

영화를 보고 싶어요.

영화를 보다

책을 읽다

음악을 듣다

불고기를 먹다

옷을 사다

Discussing length of time

TRACK 14

A 얼마 동안 계실 거예요?

B 오월 십 일부터 삼 일 동안 있을 거예요.

A How long are you going to stay?

B I am going to stay for three days from May 10.

Grammar Points

N 동안

'동안' denotes the duration of an event or state.

한 시간 동안
삼 일 동안

▶ Grammar Reference p.140

Practice

1 Look at the picture and complete the sentence using '동안'.

5 MAY

S	M	T	W	T	F	S
		1	2	3	4	5
6	7	8	9	10	11	12
13	14	15	16	17	18	19
20	21	22	23	24	25	26
27	28	29	30	31		

시험 (2–4)
1) 세일 (11–15)
2) 방학 (20–26)
3) 여행 (20–23)

삼 일 동안 시험이에요.

1) ____________ 세일이에요.

2) ____________ 방학이에요.

3) ____________ 여행을 가요.

Grammar Points

N부터

Together with time-related words such as hour, date, day, etc., '부터' shows the beginning point of time. '까지' indicates the ending point.

6시부터 9시까지
월요일부터 금요일까지

▶ Grammar Reference p.140

2 Complete the sentence using '부터' and '까지'.

오늘~내일 : 집에 있다 → 오늘부터 내일까지 집에 있을 거예요.

1) 1월~3월 : 한국어를 배우다 → ____________.

2) 월요일~금요일 : 미국을 여행하다 → ____________.

3) 10일~15일 : 한국에 있다 → ____________.

4) 7시~9시 : 영화를 보다 → ____________.

Answer **1** 1) 오 일 동안 2) 일주일 동안 3) 사 일 동안 **2** 1) 일월부터 삼월까지 한국어를 배울 거예요 2) 월요일부터 금요일까지 미국을 여행할 거예요 3) 십 일부터 십오 일까지 한국에 있을 거예요 4) 일곱 시부터 아홉 시까지 영화를 볼 거예요

Asking about something

TRACK 14

A 요금이 어떻게 돼요?

B 하루에 오만 원이에요.

A How much is the fare?

B It is 50,000 won per day.

A 전화번호가 어떻게 되세요?

B 팔팔공의 오사팔팔이에요.

A What is your phone number?

B It is 880-5488.

Notes

When you ask about personal information such as name, age and address or fare/price, "어떻게 돼요?" can be used.

Notes

'하루에' means 'per day'.

Notes

When telling telephone numbers, read each digit number like 일, 이, 삼, 사. And read '–' as '의' which can be pronounced as [에] and read '0' as '공'.

Conversation Drills 대화 연습

Conversation 1

TRACK 15

A I'd like to reserve a plane ticket.
B Where are you going?
A I am going to London.
B When are you leaving?
A I am going to leave on January 15.
B Please wait a moment. We have a flight departing at 10 o'clock in the morning.
A Then I'd like to reserve that plane.

A 비행기 표를 예약하고 싶은데요.

B 어디로 가실 거예요?

A 런던으로 갈 거예요.

B 언제 출발하실 거예요?

A 일월 십오 일에 출발할 거예요.

B 잠깐만 기다리세요. 오전 열 시 비행기가 있어요.

A 그럼 그 비행기를 예약해 주세요.

Check it

1. 런던에 갈 거예요.
   T F

2. 오후 비행기를 예약했어요.
   T F

Answer 1. T 2. F

Role-play the dialogue with your partner between a travel agent and a customer using the information below.

손님 A

1)	런던 1월 15일	2)	뉴욕 3월 27일
3)	도쿄 7월 30일	4)	방콕 12월 8일

직원 B

런던	10:00
뉴욕	21:00
도쿄	15:00
방콕	09:00

Conversation 2

TRACK 15

A Can I reserve a room now?
B Yes. For how long are you going to stay?
A From May 10, I am going to stay for three days.
B We have a room with a bed and a hot-floored room.
A Give me a room with a bed. How much is the charge?
B It's 100,000 won per day. May I have your name?
A It is Michael Johnson.

A 지금 방 예약할 수 있어요?
B 네. 얼마 동안 계실 거예요?
A 오월 십 일부터 삼 일 동안 있을 거예요.
B 침대 방하고 온돌방이 있는데요.
A 침대 방을 주세요. 요금이 어떻게 돼요?
B 하루에 십만 원이에요. 성함이 어떻게 되세요?
A 마이클 존슨이에요.

Check it

1. 마이클 씨는 온돌방에서 잘 거예요. T F
2. 마이클 씨는 5월 3일부터 호텔에 있을 거예요. T F

Answer 1. F 2. F

Role-play the dialogue between a receptionist at a hotel and a guest.

1)	2)	3)	4)
5월 10일 3일 침대 방	8월 24일 5일 침대 방	10월 6일 4일 온돌방	11월 27일 1주일 온돌방
10만원	12만원	15만원	8만원
마이클 존슨	?	?	?

Tasks & Activities 과제

Group Work

Ask your classmates from different countries about the following topics, and fill in the blanks with the information.

A 한국에서 몇 살부터 운전할 수 있어요?

B 열여덟 살부터 할 수 있어요.

운전하다

결혼하다

술을 마시다

투표하다

담배를 피우다

	한국			
운전	18살			
결혼	18살			
투표	19살			
술	19살			
담배	19살			

Listening 듣기

TRACK 16

1. Listen carefully and check(✓) on the things the person wants to do.

(　　　)

(　　　)

(　　　)

(　　　)

(　　　)

2. Listen carefully and fill in the blanks with the information.

파리	도쿄	로마	베이징	방콕	마드리드	뉴욕

1)
어디로 : 파리
출발 : ____월 ____일
(오전/오후) 9 시 30 분
요금 : ________원

2)
어디로 : ________
출발 : 6 월 3 일
(오전/오후) ____시 ____분
요금 : ________원

3)
어디로 : ________
출발 : ____월 ____일
(오전/오후) ____시 ____분
요금 : 190 만 원

3. Listen carefully and mark O for True, and mark X for False.

1) 6월 7일까지 있을 거예요. (　　)

2) 침대 방을 예약했어요. (　　)

Answer 1.

(　) (✓) (✓) (　) (　)

2. 1) 2, 15, 150만 2) 방콕, 오후, 3, 20, 37만 3) 뉴욕, 9, 23, 오전, 7, 10　3. 1) O 1) X

Reading & Writing 읽기와 쓰기

1. Read the following and mark O for True, and mark X for False.

Subject	일본에서 만나요.
Date	2006/05/13 Friday AM 11:48:14
From	yj1980@snu.co.kr
To	misako@lei.com
Cc	
Attachment	

미사코 씨에게

저는 5월 22일에 도쿄에 갈 거예요.

인천공항에서 오전 11시 비행기를 탈 거예요.

오후 1시에 공항에 도착할 거예요.

그리고 도쿄호텔에 갈 거예요.

저녁에 시내에서 미사코 씨를 만나고 싶어요.

시간 있어요?

저한테 이메일을 보내 주세요.

영준

1) 영준 씨는 이 이메일을 5월 13일에 보냈어요. (　　)

2) 영준 씨는 비행기로 일본에 갈 거예요. (　　)

3) 영준 씨는 미사코 씨를 1시에 공항에서 만날 거예요. (　　)

2. **Yeongjun is making a reservation with a travel agent on the phone. Using the information provided on the previous page complete the dialogue below.**

1) ______________________________.

2) ______________________________.

어디로 가실 거예요?

3) ______________________________.

언제 출발하실 거예요?

4) ______________________________.

잠깐만 기다리세요.
오전 11시 비행기가 있어요.

Now I can...

- ☐ make a reservation
- ☐ talk about what I want to do
- ☐ talk about possibility or ability

in Korean.

Answer **1.** 1) O 2) O 3) X **2.** 1) 비행기 표를 예약하고 싶은데요 2) 도쿄에 갈 거예요 3) 오월 이십이 일에 출발할 거예요 4) 그 비행기를 예약해 주세요

Additional Expressions 추가 표현

Types of tickets

왕복

편도

Types of rooms according to the number of occupants

일 인실

이 인실

Changing a reservation and getting a refund for a ticket

환불해 주세요. I'd like to get this refunded.

8시 표로 바꿔 주세요. I'd like to change this ticket to 8 o'clock one.

UNIT 6

Etiquette
예의

In This Unit

- Expressing permissions 허가 표현하기
- Expressing prohibitions 금지 표현하기
- Expressing a point of time 발생 시점 표현하기

Expressions 표현

그럼요.	Of course. / Certainly. / Sure.
물론이지요.	Certainly. / Of course.
네, 괜찮아요.	It's alright. / No problem.
저기요.	Excuse me.
안 되는데요.	It's not alright.
그래요? 몰랐어요.	Is that so? I didn't know.
죄송합니다.	I am sorry.

Vocabulary 어휘

Places

주차장 parking lot
기숙사 dormitory

Emotion

심심하다 bored
슬프다 sad

Verbs

들어가다 to go in / to enter
이야기하다 to talk
쓰다 to wear / to put on (a hat)
드시다 to eat (honorific)
벗다 to take off
악수하다 to shake hands
사용하다 to use
세우다 to stop

Nouns

신발 shoes
뒷사람 person behind
이용 use
차 car
기분 feeling
아기 baby
안내 information / guide
고등학생 high school student
아이 child
밖 outside

Others

그런데 but / by the way
다른 other

Words that go together

기분이 좋다 to feel good

Key Dialogues 핵심 대화

Expressing permissions

TRACK 17

A 여기에 앉아도 돼요?

B 네, 앉아도 돼요.

A May I seat here?

B Yes.

A 여기에서 음식을 먹어도 돼요?

B 그럼요.

A May I eat food here?

B Of course.

Grammar Points

V-아도/어도 되다

'-아도/어도 되다' is used to express permission. In a question, this pattern is used to ask permission from another person. In a declarative sentence, it expresses the permission of the speaker.

verb stem's last vowels ending with 'ㅏ' or 'ㅗ' + -아도 돼요 : 가다 → 가도 돼요

verbs ending with '하다', 하다 → 해도 돼요 : 전화하다 → 전화 해도 돼요

In all other cases, add '-어도 돼요' : 먹다 → 먹어도 돼요

▶ Grammar Reference p.140

Notes

When giving a full agreement, expressions such as "그럼요.", "물론이지요.", "네, 괜찮아요." are used.

Practice

Change the following verbs into '-아도/어도 돼요' pattern.

가다 → 가도 돼요

1) 먹다 → ____________ 2) 운동하다 → ____________

3) 읽다 → ____________ 4) 보다 → ____________

5) 마시다 → ____________ 6) 배우다 → ____________

Answer 1) 먹어도 돼요 2) 운동해도 돼요 3) 읽어도 돼요 4) 봐도 돼요 5) 마셔도 돼요 6) 배워도 돼요

Expressing prohibitions (1)

TRACK 17

Grammar Points

V-(으)면 안 되다

'-(으)면 안 되다' is used to express prohibition.

verb stems ending with a vowel + -면 안 돼요:
가다 → 가면 안 돼요

verb stems ending with a consonant + -으면 안 돼요:
먹다 → 먹으면 안 돼요

▶ Grammar Reference p.141

A 사진을 찍어도 돼요?
B 아니요, 찍으면 안 돼요.

A May I take a picture?
B No, you shouldn't take a picture.

Practice

● Change the following into '-(으)면 안 돼요' pattern.

음식을 먹으면 안 돼요. (음식을 먹다)

1) ______________________. (술을 마시다)

2) ______________________. (자전거를 타다)

3) ______________________. (휴대 전화를 사용하다)

4) ______________________. (교실에 들어가다)

Answer 1) 술을 마시면 안 돼요 2) 자전거를 타면 안 돼요 3) 휴대 전화를 사용하면 안 돼요 4) 교실에 들어가면 안 돼요

Expressing prohibitions (2)

TRACK 17

Notes

When calling someone's attention, "저기요." is used, which means "Excuse me," in English.

Notes

To politely say 'no' when someone asks for permission, "안 되는데요." is used.

A 저기요.

B 네?

A 여기에서 담배를 피우면 안 되는데요.

B 네. 알겠습니다.

A Excuse me.

B Yes?

A You shouldn't smoke here.

B All right.

Expressing a point of time

TRACK 17

A 한국에서는 집에 들어갈 때 신발을 벗어요.

B 그래요? 몰랐어요.

A In Korea, we take off our shoes when we go into a house.

B Is that so? I didn't know.

A 시험 볼 때 이야기하면 안 돼요.

B 죄송합니다.

A You shouldn't be talking when you're taking a test.

B I am sorry.

Grammar Points

A/V-(으)ㄹ 때

'-(으)ㄹ 때' is used, when you describe general occasions.

verb or adjective stems ending with a vowel + -ㄹ 때 : 들어가다→들어갈 때

verb or adjective stems ending with a consonant + -을 때 : 먹다→먹을 때

▶ Grammar Reference p.141

Notes

"그래요? 몰랐어요." is used when expressing that one has just found that out.

Practice

Complete the sentences using the expressions in the box.

날씨가 좋다
슬프다
기분이 좋다
어머니가 보고 싶다
기분이 안 좋다
심심하다
밥을 먹다

날씨가 좋을 때 산에 가요.

1) ______________________ 텔레비전을 봐요.

2) ______________________ 여자 친구한테 전화해요.

3) ______________________ 편지를 보내요.

4) ______________________ 이야기하면 안 돼요.

Conversation Drills 대화 연습

Conversation 1 TRACK 18

A Excuse me. May I eat food here?
B Yes, of course.
A May I smoke?
B You may not smoke.
A May I change seats?
B It's alright.

A 여기에서 음식을 먹어도 돼요?

B 네, 물론이지요.

A 담배를 피워도 돼요?

B 담배를 피우면 안 되는데요.

A 자리를 바꿔도 돼요?

B 네, 괜찮아요.

Check it

Choose what may be ok to do.

1. 음식을 먹어요. T F
2. 담배를 피워요. T F
3. 자리를 바꿔요. T F

Answer 1. T 2. F 3. T

Role-play the dialogue with your partner using the pictures below as cues.

사진을 찍다

이야기하다

밥을 먹다

술을 마시다

담배를 피우다

자다

Conversation 2

TRACK 18

A May I eat food while I am watching a movie?

B Yes, of course. But you should not take pictures.

A Really? I didn't know.

A 영화 볼 때 음식을 먹어도 돼요?

B 네, 그럼요. 그런데 사진을 찍으면 안 돼요.

A 그래요? 몰랐어요.

Check it

1. 영화 볼 때 음식을 먹어도 괜찮아요. [T] [F]
2. 영화 볼 때 사진을 찍어도 괜찮아요. [T] [F]

Answer 1. [T] 2. [F]

Role-play the dialogue with your partner using the sentences provided below.

극장에서 영화를 볼 때	밥을 먹을 때	도서관에서 공부할 때
음식을 먹다	텔레비전을 보다	옆 사람하고 이야기하다
사진을 찍다	신문을 읽다	전화하다
담배를 피우다	젓가락으로 밥을 먹다	자다
술을 마시다	______________	______________

Tasks & Activities 과제

Group Work

Ask your classmates about whether or not the following activities are allowed in their countries. Fill in the last row with your own question.

질문 \ 나라	한국		
버스 안에서 전화하다	○		
아버지 앞에서 담배를 피우다	×		
아버지 앞에서 술을 마시다	○		
여자가 남자하고 악수하다	○		
남자가 치마를 입다	×		
고등학생이 결혼하다	○		

Listening 듣기

TRACK 19

1. What shouldn't he do? Connect with the right sign.

1) ●

2) ●

3) ●

① 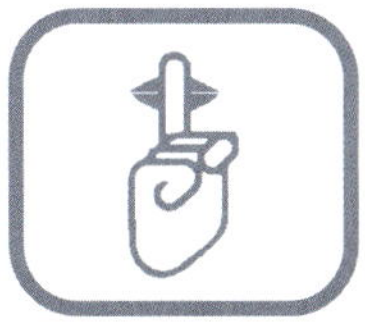

② 

③ 

④ 

2. You are invited to a friend's house. Check(√) on what you may do.

1) 

( )

2) 

( )

3) 

( )

TRACK 19

3. **Why shouldn't the person do the following? Listen and write down the number of the corresponding picture.**

1) (　　)　　2) (　　)　　3) (　　)　　4) (　　)

① 

② 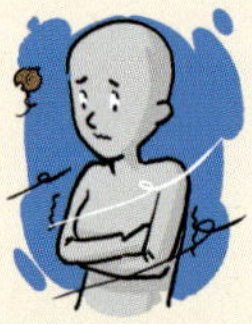

③ 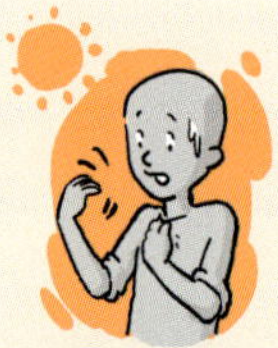

④ 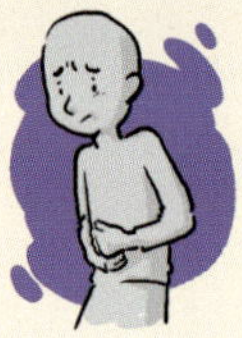

⑤ 

⑥ 

4. **What does he do when he is in the following mood? Match the moods with the activities.**

1) 

2) 

3) 

4) 

① 

② 

③ 

④ 

⑤ 

Answer **1.** 1) ④ 2) ① 3) ③ **2.** 1) √ 2) √ **3.** 1) ② 2) ⑤ 3) ⑥ 4) ① **4.** 1) ⑤ 2) ③ 3) ① 4) ②

Reading & Writing 읽기와 쓰기

1. **The following shows the dos and don'ts at a library. Read and see if the following sentences below the box correspond with the directions in the box. Mark O if they do, and X if they don't.**

> **도서관 이용 안내**
>
> 1. 도서관 안에서 휴대 전화를 사용하면 안 돼요.
> 2. 도서관 안에서 음식을 먹으면 안 돼요. 도서관 앞에 식당이 있어요. 그 식당에서 음식을 드세요.
> 3. 도서관 안에서 담배를 피우면 안 돼요. 도서관 밖에서 담배를 피우세요.
> 4. 도서관 앞에 차를 세우면 안 돼요. 도서관 뒤에 주차장이 있어요. 그 주차장에 차를 세우세요.

1) 도서관 안에서 전화해도 돼요. (X)

2) 도서관 안에서 밥을 먹을 수 있어요. ( )

3) 도서관 밖에서 담배를 피워도 돼요. ( )

4) 도서관 뒤에 차를 세울 수 있어요. ( )

2. **Referring to the information given on the previous page, make a set of rules on how to use a dormitory.**

기숙사 이용 안내

1. ____.

2. ____.

3. ____.

4. ____.

Now I can...

- ☐ express permissions
- ☐ express prohibitions
- ☐ express a point of time

in Korean.

Answer 1. 1) X 2) X 3) O 4) O

Additional Expressions 추가 표현

Manners that should be kept in Korea

어른에게 한 손으로 물건을 드리면 안 돼요.
You shouldn't give something to elders with one hand.
(When you give something to elders, you should use your both hands.)

어른 앞에서 담배를 피우면 안 돼요.
You shouldn't smoke in front of elders.

집 안에서 신발을 신으면 안 돼요.
You shouldn't wear shoes in the house.

그릇을 들고 밥을 먹으면 안 돼요.
You shouldn't hold up the bowls while eating.

어른보다 먼저 숟가락을 들면 안 돼요.
You shouldn't start eating before elders do.

밥 먹을 때 코를 풀면 안 돼요.
You shouldn't blow your nose during the meal.

UNIT 7

Hospital

병원

In This Unit

- Describing symptoms 증세 표현하기
- Talking about causes and reasons 원인, 이유 표현하기
- Expressing prohibitions 금지 표현하기

Expressions 표현

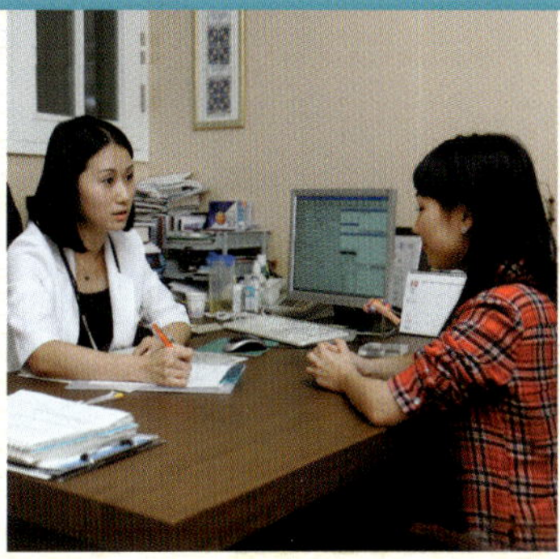

어떻게 오셨어요?	What brought you here? / What brings you here?
어디가 아파요?	Where does it hurt?
머리가 아파서 왔어요.	I came because my head hurts.
이 약을 드세요.	Take this medicine.

Vocabulary 어휘

Body

몸 body
머리 head
어깨 shoulder
귀 ear
발 foot
허리 waist
다리 leg
팔 arm
배 abdomen / stomach
눈 eye
코 nose
목 neck / throat
손 hand

Adjectives

아프다 ill / in pain / hurt
크다 big

Others

감기 cold
다치다 to be hurt
기침 cough
열 fever
나다 to have (a fever / a runny nose)
피 blood
콧물 runny nose
찬물 cold water
땀 sweat
그래서 so
지난 last
스키장 ski resort
넘어지다 fall down
매일 everyday
일기 diary

Words that go together

감기에 걸리다 to catch a cold
기침을 하다 to have a cough
열이 나다 to have a fever
콧물이 나다 to have a runny nose

Key Dialogues 핵심 대화

Explaining where it hurts

TRACK 20

A 어디가 아파요?

B 머리가 아파요.

A Where does it hurt?

B My head hurts.

Grammar Points

'ㅡ' irregular verbs & adjectives

When verbs and adjectives with vowel ending 'ㅡ' in their stem meet '–아/어–', 'ㅡ' is dropped and '–아–' or '–어–' is added.

'–아–' is added when the stem has either 'ㅏ' or 'ㅗ', as in the following examples.

바쁘다 : 바쁘 + –아요 → 바빠요
배고프다 : 배고프 + –아서 → 배고파서

In other cases, '–어–' is added.

예쁘다 : 예쁘 + –어요 → 예뻐요
쓰다 : 쓰 + –어서 → 써서

▶ Grammar Reference p.141

Practice

1 Fill in the blanks with proper forms of the given verbs and adjectives.

	–(으)면	–아요/어요	–았어요/었어요	–아서/어서
바쁘다	바쁘면	1)	바빴어요	바빠서
아프다	2)	아파요	3)	아파서
배고프다	배고프면	배고파요	배고팠어요	4)
예쁘다	5)	예뻐요	6)	예뻐서
쓰다	쓰면	7)	썼어요	써서
크다	크면	커요	컸어요	8)

Grammar Points

N이/가 아프다

When expressing where you feel the pain, '이/가 아프다' is added to the part of body.

머리가 아파요.
목이 아파요.

▶ Grammar Reference p.142

2 Practice the dialogue with your partner using the given pictures as cues.

1) ______. 2) ______. 3) ______.

Answer **1** 1) 바빠요 2) 아프면 3) 아팠어요 4) 배고파서 5) 예쁘면 6) 예뻤어요 7) 써요 8) 커서 **2** 1) 눈이 아파요 2) 팔이 아파요 3) 허리가 아파요

Explaining why one came to see the doctor

TRACK 20

A 어떻게 오셨어요?

B 감기에 걸려서 왔어요.

A How can I help you?

B I came because I caught a cold.

Notes

When asking the reason for coming to see the doctor, "어떻게 오셨어요?" is used.

Notes

When saying one caught a disease, '에 걸렸어요' is added to the name of disease.

감기에 걸렸어요.
눈병에 걸렸어요.

A 어떻게 오셨어요?

B 다리를 다쳐서 왔어요.

A How can I help you?

B I came because I had hurt my leg.

Notes

When talking about the body part that you have hurt, '을/를 다치다' is added to the part of body.

다리를 다쳤어요.
팔을 다쳤어요.

Describing symptoms

TRACK 20

A 어떻게 아프세요?

B 기침을 많이 해요.

A How does it hurt?

B I cough a lot.

Notes

When asking about symptoms, "어떻게 아프세요?" is used.

A 어떻게 아프세요?

B 기침을 많이 해요. 그리고 열도 나요.

A How does it hurt?

B I cough a lot and I have a fever, too.

Notes

Expressions for symptoms are as follows.

기침을 해요.
열이 나요.
콧물이 나요.
피가 나요.

Grammar Points

N도

'도' is used to express the meaning of 'also'.

▶ Grammar Reference p.142

Practice

Practice the dialogue with your partner using '도'.

어떻게 아프세요?

 기침 +  콧물

기침을 해요.
그리고 콧물도 나요.

1) 어디가 아프세요?  머리 +  목

2) 누구를 좋아해요?  아버지 +  어머니

3) 뭘 먹었어요?  불고기 +  냉면

Answer 1) 머리가 아파요. 그리고 목도 아파요. 2) 아버지를 좋아해요. 그리고 어머니도 좋아해요. 3) 불고기를 먹었어요. 그리고 냉면도 먹었어요.

Giving a reason

TRACK 20

Grammar Points

A/V-(으)니까

'-(으)니까' means 'because', 'since' or 'so'.

verb or adjective stems ending with a vowel + -니까
: 보다 → 보니까

verb or adjective stems ending with a consonant + -으니까 : 먹다 → 먹으니까

▶ Grammar Reference p.142

A 무슨 약을 먹어야 돼요?

B 감기에 걸렸으니까 이 약을 드세요.

A What medicine should I take?

B Since you got a cold, take this medicine.

Practice

Find the matching pictures for the sentence below and complete the sentences using '-(으)니까'.

덥다

춥다

돈이 없다

일이 많다

배고프다

길이 복잡하다

더우니까 아이스크림을 먹을까요?

1) ____________________ 물을 많이 드세요.

2) ____________________ 쉬세요.

3) ____________________ 지하철을 타요.

4) ____________________ 식당에 갈까요?

Expressing prohibitions

TRACK 20

Grammar Points

V-지 마세요

'-지 마세요' is the negative imperative form.

가다 → 가지 마세요
앉다 → 앉지 마세요

▶ Grammar Reference p.143

A 수영해도 돼요?

B 감기에 걸렸으니까 수영하지 마세요.

A May I swim?

B Since you have a cold, don't swim.

Practice

Talk about the signs with your partner using '-지 마세요'.

1)  사진을 찍다 ______________________.

2)  담배를 피우다 ______________________.

3)  들어가다 ______________________.

4)  전화하다 ______________________.

5)  음료수를 마시다 ______________________.

Answer 1) 사진을 찍지 마세요 2) 담배를 피우지 마세요 3) 들어가지 마세요 4) 전화하지 마세요 5) 음료수를 마시지 마세요

Conversation Drills 대화 연습

Conversation

TRACK 21

A How can I help you?
B I came because my head hurts.
A Sit here, please. Since when have you been sick?
B I have been sick since yesterday.
...
A You caught a cold, so don't drink cold water. And you have to rest a lot.
B Should I come again tomorrow?
A Yes, come again tomorrow, please.

A 어떻게 오셨어요?

B 머리가 아파서 왔어요.

A 여기 앉으세요. 언제부터 아팠어요?

B 어제부터 아팠어요.

• • •

A 감기에 걸렸으니까 찬물을 마시지 마세요. 그리고 많이 쉬세요.

B 내일 다시 와야 돼요?

A 네, 내일 다시 오세요.

Check it

1. 이 사람은 어디가 아파요?
   ① 머리 ② 다리

2. 이 사람은 뭘 하면 안 돼요?
   ① ②

Answer 1. ① 2. ②

Role-play the dialogue with your partner. Use the following expressions.

B 머리가 아프다 / 열이 나다 / 기침이 나다 / 배가 아프다

A 찬물을 마시다 / 일을 많이 하다 / 노래하다 / 아이스크림을 먹다 / 수영하다 / 운동하다

Tasks & Activities 과제

Group Work

Role a die and make a sentence using the expression in the box and '-(으)니까'.
If you fail to make a sentence, you have to go back to where you roll the die before.

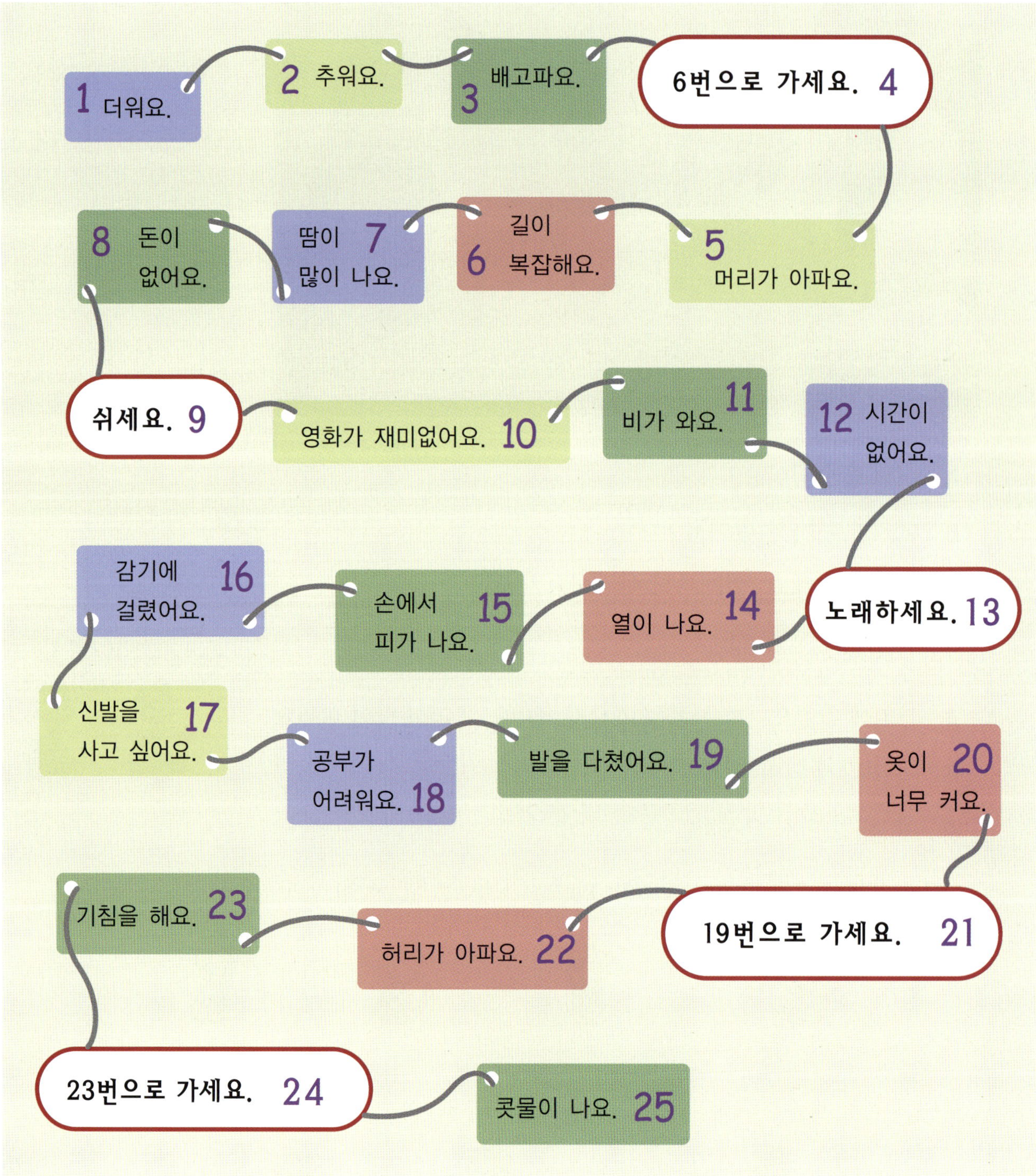

Listening 듣기

TRACK 22

1. Listen carefully and find out what one should not do, and then connect with the corresponding picture.

1) 2) 3) 4) 5)

① ② ③ ④ ⑤ ⑥

2. Listen carefully and write down the number which best describes the symptoms.

1) ________ 2) ________ 3) ________

① ② ③ ④ ⑤ ⑥

3. Listen carefully and check(✓) on the correct answer.

1) ① 배가 아파서 ② 이가 아파서 ③ 감기에 걸려서

2) ①

②

③

Answer 1. 1) ④ 2) ⑤ 3) ⑥ 4) ③ 5) ① 2. 1) ④ 2) ③ 3) ⑥ 3. 1) ③ 2) ③

Reading & Writing 읽기와 쓰기

1. Read the following passages, and connect each passage with the correct picture.

1) 나는 어제 날씨가 너무 더워서 아이스크림을 많이 먹었어요. 그래서 배가 많이 아팠어요. ● ① 

2) 나는 지난 주말에 스키장에 갔어요. 그런데 넘어져서 다리를 다쳤어요. 다리가 많이 아팠어요. ● ② 

3) 나는 일요일에 수영장에 갔어요. 날씨가 추웠지만 수영을 했어요. 그래서 감기에 걸렸어요. 기침을 많이 해요. 그리고 머리도 아파요. ● ③ 

2. Have you ever sick or hurt? Write about your experiences.

Now I can...

- ☐ describe symptoms
- ☐ explain causes and reasons
- ☐ express prohibitions

in Korean.

Answer 1. 1) ③ 2) ② 3) ①

Additional Expressions 추가 표현

Useful expressions when describing symptoms and causes of sickness

소화가 안 돼요.
My stomach is upset.

속이 안 좋아요.
I feel something wrong inside.

토해요.
I throw up.

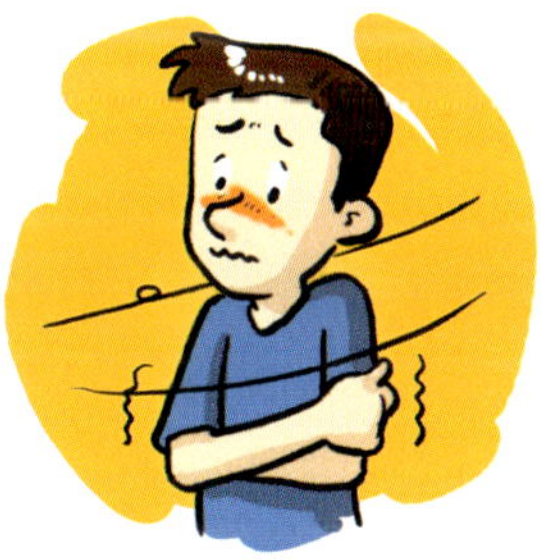

몸살이 났어요.
I suffer from fatigue.

손을 데었어요.
I got a burn in the hand.

발목을 삐었어요.
I sprained my ankle.

다리가 부러졌어요.
I broke my leg.

멍이 들었어요.
I got a bruise.

이가 썩었어요.
I have a cavity (in a tooth).

UNIT 8

Advice & Suggestions
충고와 제안

In This Unit

- Asking for and giving advice 조언하기
- Making suggestions 권유하기

Expressions 표현

그게 좋겠어요.	That would be good. / That sounds good.
그거 좋은 생각이에요.	That's a good idea.
어디 아파요?	You look sick. Are you alright?
무슨 일 있어요?	Is something wrong?
무슨 걱정 있어요?	Is something wrong?

Vocabulary 어휘

Nouns

요가 yoga
건강 health
약 medicine
살 flesh
걱정 worry / concern
생각 thinking / thought
등산 mountain climbing / hiking
다이어트 diet
한라산 Hallasan
윷놀이 yunnori
피라미드 pyramid
에펠탑 the Eiffel Tower
생선회 sliced raw fish
고민 agony / worry
말하기 speaking
집안일 chores

Others

찌다 to gain (weight)
한번 once
특히 especially
이렇게 like this / in this way
자주 often
잘하다 be good at
도와주다 to help
그렇지만 but
항상 always
내다 to pay
멀다 far
길다 long

Words that go together

살이 찌다 to gain weight

Key Dialogues 핵심 대화

Asking for and giving advice

TRACK 23

A 여자들한테 무슨 운동이 좋아요?

B 요가가 여자들한테 좋아요.

A What exercise is good for women?

B Yoga is good for women.

Grammar Points

N은/는 N′한테 좋다/나쁘다

This expression means that N is good/bad for N′. When N′ is a person or an animal, '한테' is used after N′.

이 음식은 아기한테 좋아요.

▶ Grammar Reference p.143

A 담배 있어요?

B 담배는 건강에 나빠요.

A Do you have a cigarette?

B Cigarette is not good for your health.

Grammar Points

N은/는 N′에 좋다/나쁘다

When N′ is an inanimated thing, '에' is used after N′.

이 음식은 몸에 좋아요.

▶ Grammar Reference p.143

Practice

Using the words below make as many sentences as possible.

이 약은 여자한테 좋아요. | 담배는 건강에 나빠요.

1) 이 약

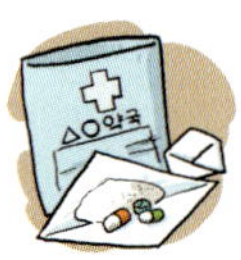

2) 담배

3) 술

4) 이 운동

5) 이 책

6) 커피

- 아이들
- 건강
- 감기
- 여자

Making suggestions (1)

TRACK 23

A 어디가 아파요?

B 감기에 걸렸어요.

A 그럼 병원에 가 보세요.

A Where does it hurt?

B I caught a cold.

A Well then, go to the hospital.

Grammar Points

V-아/어 보세요

'V-아/어 보세요' is a sentence ending denoting a suggestion or recommendation. This can be used when politely inducing someone to try something.

verb stem's final vowels ending with 'ㅏ' or 'ㅗ' + -아 보세요 : 가다 → 가 보세요

verbs ending with '하다', 하다 → 해 보세요 : 수영하다 → 수영해 보세요

In all other cases, add '-어 보세요' : 먹다 → 먹어 보세요

▶ Grammar Reference p.143

Practice

Making suggestions as shown in the example below.

이 차를 마셔 보세요.

1) 운동 

________________.

2) 불고기 

________________.

3) 책 

________________.

4) 제주도 

________________.

Answer 1) 운동을 해 보세요 2) 불고기를 먹어 보세요 3) 책을 읽어 보세요 4) 제주도에 가 보세요

Making suggestions (2)

TRACK 23

A 어디 아파요?

B 감기에 걸렸어요.

A 그럼 좀 쉬세요.

A You look sick. Are you alright?

B I caught a cold.

A Then, why don't you get some rest?

Notes

When someone looks sick or worried, "어디 아파요?" or "무슨 일 있어요?" is used.

Notes

When talking about the reason for one's concerns, the pattern '-아서/어서 걱정이에요' is used.

돈이 없어서 걱정이에요.
내일 시험이 있어서 걱정이에요.

A 왜 밥을 안 먹어요? 무슨 일 있어요?

B 요즘 살이 쪄서 걱정이에요.

A 그럼 매일 운동을 해 보세요.

A Why are you not eating? Is something wrong?

B I'm worried because I gained weight these days.

A Well then, try exercising everyday.

Making suggestions (3)

TRACK 23

Grammar Points

V–는 게 어때요?

This expression is used when suggesting something.

병원에 가는 게 어때요?

▶ Grammar Reference p.144

A 요즘 살이 많이 쪘어요.

B 운동하는 게 어때요?

A I gained a lot of weight lately.

B Why don't you exercise?

Practice

Look at the pictures below and make suggestions using '–는 게 어때요?'.

1) 

________________?

2) 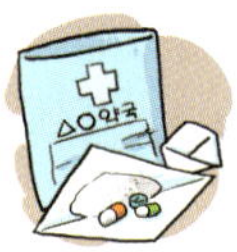

________________?

3) 

________________?

4) 

________________?

Answer 1) 병원에 가는 게 어때요 2) 약을 먹는 게 어때요 3) 차를 마시는 게 어때요 4) 자는 게 어때요

Making suggestions (4)

TRACK 23

A 무슨 음식을 만들까요?

B 불고기를 만드는 게 어때요?

A 그게 좋겠어요.

A What food shall we make?

B How about making bulgogi?

A That would be good.

Grammar Points

'ㄹ' irregular verbs & adjectives

When a verb or adjective stem with 'ㄹ' is followed by endings beginning with 'ㄴ', 'ㅂ', or 'ㅅ', the stem's 'ㄹ' is dropped. And also in this case, '-(으)' which is supposed to be added to the stem with consonant ending is also dropped.

저는 지금 불고기를 만드는데요.

▶ Grammar Reference p.144

Notes

When agreeing to someone's suggestion, "그게 좋겠어요." or "그거 좋은 생각이에요." is used.

Practice

Fill in the blanks with the correct forms of each verb.

	-아요/어요	-(으)니까	-(으)면	-는데요
만들다	만들어요	1)	만들면	2)
살다	3)	사니까	4)	5)
알다	6)	7)	8)	아는데요

Answer 1) 만드니까 2) 만드는데요 3) 살아요 4) 살면 5) 사는데요 6) 알아요 7) 아니까 8) 알면

Conversation Drills 대화 연습

Conversation 1 TRACK 24

A Annie, is something wrong?
B I gained a lot of weight lately.
A Well then, try hiking.
Hiking is very good for your diet.
B Is that so? Thanks.

A 애니 씨, 무슨 걱정 있어요?

B 요즘 살이 많이 쪘어요.

A 그럼 등산을 해 보세요. 등산은 다이어트에 아주 좋아요.

B 그래요? 고마워요.

Check it

1. 애니 씨는 감기에 걸렸어요.
   T F
2. 등산은 다이어트에 좋아요.
   T F

Answer 1. F 2. T

Role-play the dialogue with your partner using the following words and expressions.

1) 요즘 살이 많이 찌다
등산을 하다
등산 / 다이어트

2) 한국어가 어렵다
이 책을 읽다
이 책 / 한국어 공부

3) 목이 너무 아프다
차를 마시다
차 / 목

Conversation 2

TRACK 24

A 영준 씨, 왜 그래요? 어디 아파요?

B 요즘 일이 많아서 너무 피곤해요.

A 그럼 좀 쉬는 게 어때요?

B 일이 많아서 쉴 수 없어요.

A 그럼 차를 마셔 보세요. 차는 몸에 아주 좋아요.

B 그게 좋겠어요. 고마워요.

A Yeongjun, what's wrong? Are you sick?

B I am so tired because I have a lot of work these days.

A Then, why don't you take a break?

B I can't because there is a lot of work (to do).

A Well then, try drinking tea. Tea is very good for your health.

B That will be good. Thanks.

Check it

1. 영준 씨는 아파서 일을 할 수 없어요. T F

2. 영준 씨는 시간이 없어서 차를 못 마셔요. T F

Answer 1. F 2. F

Role-play the dialogue with your partner using the following words and expressions.

1)	2)	3)
요즘 일이 많다 / 피곤하다	감기에 걸리다 / 머리가 아프다	말을 많이 하다 / 목이 아프다
좀 쉬다	집에 가다	병원에 가다
일이 많다 / 쉬다	내일 시험이 있다 / 가다	바쁘다 / 가다
차 / 몸	오렌지 주스 / 감기	이 약 / 목

Tasks & Activities 과제

Pair work

Followings are some famous things in Korea and other countries. Using the given example as cues, introduce some food or tourist attractions of your country to your partner.

Example

비빔밥을 먹어 보세요. 아주 맛있어요.

한라산이 아주 아름다워요. 한번 가 보세요.

비빔밥

한라산

태권도

한국 드라마

김치

윷놀이

피라미드

에펠탑

피자

생선회

Listening 듣기

TRACK 25

1. Listen carefully and write down the number of the corresponding picture.

1) ______ 2) ______ 3) ______ 4) ______ 5) ______

2. Listen to the dialogue and choose the right answer.

①

②

③

3. Listen to the dialogue and choose the right answer.

1) ①  ②  ③ 

2) ① 쉬어야 돼요. ② 물을 마셔야 돼요. ③ 과일을 먹어야 돼요.

4. Listen to the dialogue and choose the right answer.

1) ① 밥을 안 먹어서 ② 밥을 너무 많이 먹어서 ③ 밥을 빨리 먹어서

2) ①  ②  ③ 

Answer 1. 1) ⑧ 2) ① 3) ⑨ 4) ④ 5) ⑥
2. ③ 3. 1) ② 2) ② 4. 1) ③ 2) ①

Reading & Writing 읽기와 쓰기

The following sentences on the left are what your friends are worried about. Read them and give an advice as the first example.

나의 고민		이렇게 해 보세요!
요즘 저는 한국어 공부가 너무 어려워서 걱정이에요. 특히 말하기가 어려워요. 어떻게 하면 좋아요?	➡	한국어 말하기가 어려우면 한국 텔레비전을 자주 보세요. 그리고 한국 친구를 만드세요. 그러면 한국어를 잘할 수 있어요.

나의 고민		이렇게 해 보세요!
저는 요즘 감기에 걸려서 많이 아파요. 회사에도 가야 돼요. 그리고 집안일도 해야 돼요. 그런데 남편이 안 도와줘요.	➡	

나의 고민		이렇게 해 보세요!
저는 우리 회사의 마이클 씨를 좋아해요. 그런데 그 사람은 애니 씨를 좋아해요. 어떻게 하면 좋아요?	➡	

나의 고민		이렇게 해 보세요!
저는 제 여자 친구를 사랑해요. 그렇지만 여자 친구를 만나면 항상 제가 돈을 내야 돼서 힘들어요.	➡	

Now I can...

- ☐ ask for and give advice
- ☐ make suggestions

in Korean.

Additional Expressions 추가 표현

Situations where advice is needed

시험에 떨어졌어요.
I failed on the test.

친구하고 싸웠어요.
I had an argument with my friend.

일이 너무 많아서 스트레스를 받아요.
Too much work gives me stress.

요즘은 자주 화가 나요.
I often get angry these days.

여자 친구하고 헤어졌어요.
I broke up with my girlfriend.

아이가 말을 안 들어요.
My child doesn't listen to me.

UNIT 9

Shopping

쇼핑

In This Unit

- Purchasing 구매하기
- Describing a noun by modifying 묘사하기
- Comparing 비교하기
- Exchanging 교환하기

Expressions 표현

뭘 찾으세요?	What are you looking for?
저 치마 좀 보여 주세요.	Please show me that skirt.
이거 한번 입어 보세요.	Try this on.
이 치마는 어때요?	How about this skirt?
이 치마는 어떠세요?	How about this skirt? (more polite)

Vocabulary 어휘

Colors

색 color
노란색 yellow
파란색 blue
까만색 black
하얀색 white
녹색 green
갈색 brown
회색 grey
빨간색 red

Adjectives

짧다 short
맛없다 untasty
무겁다 heavy
무섭다 scary
높다 high
똑똑하다 smart
낮다 low
편하다 comfortable
착하다 good-natured
힘들다 laborous / hard

Nouns

빌딩 building
달러 dollar
티셔츠 T-shirt
다음 next
지우개 eraser
야구 baseball
서울 Seoul

Verbs

찾다 to look for
바꾸다 to exchange
깎다 to discount
신다 to put on (shoes)

Others

어떤 what kind of
참 very / really
또 again / once more

Key Dialogues 핵심 대화

Buying something at a store

TRACK 26

A 어서 오세요. 뭘 찾으세요?

B 짧은 치마를 사고 싶은데요.

A Welcome. What are you looking for?

B I'd like to buy a short skirt.

Notes

"뭘 찾으세요?" is an expression used when asking what a guest wants.

Grammar Points

A-(으)ㄴ N

By adding '-(으)ㄴ' to an adjective stem and placing it in front of a noun, the adjective modifies and defines the state or characteristic of the noun.

adjective stems ending with a vowel + -ㄴ : 예쁘다 + 옷 → 예쁜 옷

adjective stems ending with a consonant + -은 : 좋다 + 약 → 좋은 약

▶ Grammar Reference p.145

Practice

Change the words below as shown in the example.

비싸다 → 비싼 옷

1) 좋다 → __________ 친구

2) 바쁘다 → __________ 사람

3) 높다 → __________ 빌딩

4) 크다 → __________ 신발

Answer 1) 좋은 2) 바쁜 3) 높은 4) 큰

Recommending something

TRACK 26

A 이 하얀색 치마는 어떠세요? 아주 예쁘고 편해요.

B 다른 색은 없어요?

A 그럼 이건 어때요?

A How about this white skirt? It is very pretty and comfortable.

B Isn't there any other color?

A Well then, how about this?

Grammar Points

S-고 S'

By using '-고' after a verb or adjective stem of first clause, two sentences of an equal status, which are enumerated using '그리고', can be combined into one.

이 치마는 싸요. 그리고 예뻐요.
= 이 치마는 싸고 예뻐요.

▶ Grammar Reference p.145

Notes

'이거는, 그거는, 저거는' can be shortened into '이건, 그건, 저건'. When particles '이/가' are added to '이거, 그거, 저거', they become '이게, 그게, 저게'. '이거, 그거, 저거' with object particle '을/를' become '이거를, 그거를, 저거를' and their short forms are '이걸, 그걸, 저걸'. In spoken Korean, the shortened forms are more often used.

Practice

Make one sentence using '-고' as shown in the example.

이 신발은 싸요. + 편해요. → 이 신발은 싸고 편해요.

1) 그 식당은 비싸요. + 맛없어요. → ______________.

2) 그 사람은 똑똑해요. + 착해요. → ______________.

3) 저 책은 쉬워요. + 재미있어요. → ______________.

4) 이 옷은 예뻐요. + 싸요. → ______________.

Notes

색

빨간색 노란색
녹색 파란색
갈색 까만색
회색 하얀색

Answer 1) 그 식당은 비싸고 맛없어요 2) 그 사람은 똑똑하고 착해요 3) 저 책은 쉽고 재미있어요 4) 이 옷은 예쁘고 싸요

Exchanging

TRACK 26

Grammar Points

N을/를 N′(으)로 바꾸다

When exchanging something for something else, use '을/를' with the preceding noun, and add '(으)로' to the following noun.

▶ Grammar Reference p.146

A 치마가 좀 긴데요. 이 치마를 다른 치마로 바꿔 주세요.

B 그럼 이건 어때요?

A The skirt is a little long. Exchange this for another skirt please.

B Then, how about this?

Practice

Make a sentence as shown in the example.

> 치마, 바지 → 치마를 바지로 바꿔 주세요.

1) 이거, 저거 → ______________________.

2) 연필, 지우개 → ______________________.

3) 이 돈, 달러 → ______________________.

4) 사과, 오렌지 → ______________________.

Answer 1) 이거를 저거로 바꿔 주세요 2) 연필을 지우개로 바꿔 주세요 3) 이 돈을 달러로 바꿔 주세요 4) 사과를 오렌지로 바꿔 주세요

Comparing

TRACK 26

A 치마가 좀 길어요.

B 그럼 이거 한번 입어 보세요. 이게 그거보다 짧아요.

A 더 짧은 거는 없어요?

A The skirt is a little long.
B Then, try this on.
This is shorter than that.
A Isn't there a shorter one?

Practice

1 Make sentences using the given pictures and 'N보다 (더) A'.

바나나가 사과보다 더 비싸요.

2 Answer the following questions using 'A-(으)ㄴ 거'.

어떤 음악 듣고 싶어요?

슬픈 거 듣고 싶어요.

1) 어떤 음식 먹고 싶어요?
2) 어떤 영화 보고 싶어요?
3) 어떤 신발 사고 싶어요?
4) 어떤 책 읽고 싶어요?

Grammar Points

N보다 (더) A

When comparing two things, the particle '보다' is added to the one, which is the basis of the comparison, and '더', which means 'more', is added in front of adjective.

야구가 축구보다 더 재미있어요.

The adverb '더' can be omitted giving no change of meaning to the sentence.

오늘이 어제보다 더 바빠요.
= 오늘이 어제보다 바빠요.

▶ Grammar Reference p.146

Grammar Points

A-(으)ㄴ 거

When a thing is already mentioned in the previous sentence, it is alright to repeat it again, but it is also alright to replace it with '거'.

A : 어떤 음식을 좋아하세요?
B : 매운 음식을 좋아해요.
= 매운 거를 좋아해요.

▶ Grammar Reference p.146

Conversation Drills 대화 연습

Conversation 1

TRACK 27

A What are you looking for?
B I'd like to buy a pair of pants.
A How about these white pants?
They are very pretty and comfortable.
B Aren't there other colors?
A Then, how about these black pants?
Why don't you try them on?

A 뭘 찾으세요?

B 바지를 사고 싶은데요.

A 이 하얀색 바지는 어때요? 아주 예쁘고 편해요.

B 다른 색은 없어요?

A 그럼 까만색 바지는 어때요? 한번 입어 보세요.

Check it

손님은 뭘 사요?

① 

② 

Answer ①

You came to buy some clothes. Role-play the dialogue with your partner using the pictures belows as cues.

1) 바지

2) 치마

3) 코트

Conversation 2

TRACK 27

A Welcome.
B The pants are a little short. Exchange them for longer pants, please.
A How about these?
B Aren't there longer pants?
A Then, how about these?

A 어서 오세요.
B 바지가 좀 짧은데요. 긴 바지로 바꿔 주세요.
A 이건 어때요?
B 더 긴 거 없어요?
A 그럼 이건 어때요?

Check it

손님은 왜 여기에 왔어요?
① 바지가 길어서
② 바지가 짧아서

Answer ②

- You came to exchange what you had bought the other day. Role-play the dialogue with your partner using the pictures below as cues.

1) 

짧다 길다

2) 

작다 크다

3) 

길다 짧다

4) 

크다 작다

Tasks & Activities 과제

Pair work

Make sentences with your partner describing the people and things in the classroom.
Use the adjectives in the box and 'N보다 (더) A' pattern.

길다	무겁다	높다	크다	어렵다
비싸다	편하다	좋다	많다	재미있다

Listening 듣기

TRACK 28

1. Listen carefully and check(✓) on the correct answer.

1)	호주	✓	일본	
2)	어제		오늘	
3)	주스		커피	
4)	토요일		일요일	
5)	사과		포도	

2. Listen carefully and choose the clothes purchased.

①  ②  ③ 

3. Listen to the following and mark O for True, and mark X for False.

1) 어제 남대문시장에 갔어요. ( )

2) 날씨가 추워서 코트를 샀어요. ( )

3) 치마가 비싸서 안 샀어요. ( )

Answer 1. 1) 호주 2) 오늘 3) 주스 4) 토요일 5) 포도 2. ③ 3. 1) O 2) X 3) X

Reading & Writing 읽기와 쓰기

1. Annie has been to Namdaemun Market and a department store. Read the following statements.

남대문시장

백화점

2. How are Namdaemun Market and the department store different? Write a paragraph explaining the differences.

Now I can...

- ☐ buy things
- ☐ describe characteristics of something
- ☐ compare two objects
- ☐ exchange a product

in Korean.

Additional Expressions 추가 표현

More expressions related to wearing

Grammar Reference 문법 설명

UNIT 1 Family

1. N의 N′

When expressing possessive case, '의' is added to possessor, N, and it can be pronounced as [에].

애니 씨의 여동생

애니의 책

Also note that '의' is often omitted.

애니 씨의 여동생 = 애니 씨 여동생
친구의 집 = 친구 집

이 사람은 애니 씨의 여동생이에요.
This is Annie's younger sister.

어제 친구 집에 갔어요.
Yesterday, I went to my friend's house.

2. N(이)세요

'-(이)세요' is a combination of '-이에요/예요' and '-(으)시-', which shows respect towards the subject.

If the noun ends with a vowel + -세요 :
아버지 → 아버지세요
If the noun ends with a consonant + -이세요 :
선생님 → 선생님이세요

이분은 우리 아버지세요. This is my father.

A : 저분이 김 선생님이세요? Is that Mr./Ms. Kim?
B : 아니요, 박 선생님이세요. No, that is Mr./Ms. Park.

3. 누구

The interrogative '누구' is used with '을/를' and '의' as in '누구를', '누구의' to indicate the case. But the combination of '누구' and subject particle '이/가' is not '누구가' but '누가'.

누구가 (X) → 누가 (O)

When answering the question with '누가', '이/가' is attached to the subject.

A : 누가 전화했어요?
B : 마이클 씨는 전화했어요. (X)
→ 마이클 씨가 전화했어요. (O)

4. A/V-(으)세요

'-(으)세요' is a combination of '-(으)시-' and the present tense sentence ending '-아요/어요'.

If the verb or adjective stem ends with a vowel + -세요
: 보다 → 보세요
If the verb or adjective stem ends with a consonant + -으세요 : 읽다 → 읽으세요

아버지는 지금 텔레비전을 보세요.
My father is watching TV, now.

어머니는 책을 읽으세요. My mother is reading a book.

A : 선생님, 어디에 가세요?
Sir/Ma'am, where are you going?
B : 집에 가요. I'm going home.

This form is also used for polite order.

집에 가세요. Please go home.

5. 무슨 N

'무슨' is used when asking someone to choose and answer from a pool of options.

A : 무슨 꽃을 좋아해요? What kind of flowers do you like?
B : 장미를 좋아해요. I like roses.

A : 오늘은 무슨 요일이에요? What day is today?
B : 수요일이에요. It's Wednesday.

'무슨' is always used with a noun, but '뭐' is always used alone.

뭐 읽어요?
무슨 책 읽어요?

6. A/V-(으)셨어요

'-(으)셨어요' is a combination of '-(으)시-' and the past tense sentence ending '-았어요/었어요'.

If the verb or adjective stem ends with a vowel + -셨어요 : 가다 → 가셨어요
If the verb or adjective stem ends with a consonant + -으셨어요 : 읽다 → 읽으셨어요

아버지는 회사에 가셨어요.	My father went to work.
어머니는 이 책을 읽으셨어요.	My mother read this book.
A : 언제 결혼하셨어요?	When did you get married?
B : 작년에 결혼했어요.	I got married last year.

UNIT 2 Transportation

1. N에서 N'을/를 타다

When expressing getting on a mode of transportation, the verb '타다' is used. '타다' requires an object and object particle '을/를'. After the place where one gets on, '에서' is attached.

버스를 타요. I take a bus.

A : 남대문시장에 어떻게 가요?
Would you tell me how to get to Namdaemun Market?
B : 학교 앞에서 버스를 타세요.
Take a bus in front of the school.

2. N에서 내리다

When expressing getting off at a place, 'N에서 내리다' is used.

A : 어디에서 내려요?	Where should I get off?
B : 회현역에서 내리세요.	Get off at Hoehyeon Station.

The particle '에서' also follows the mode of transportation meaning 'from'.

버스에서 내려요. I get off a bus.

3. N에서 N'(으)로 갈아타다

When expressing transferring, the verb '갈아타다' is used. '(으)로' comes after the mode of transportation one transfer to. '에서' follows the place where one transfers.

명동에서 버스로 갈아탔어요.
I transferred to a bus at Myeong-dong.

A : 어디에서 갈아타요?
Where should I transfer?
B : 교대역에서 삼 호선으로 갈아타세요.
Transfer to line 3 at Seoul Nat'l Univ. of Education Station.

4. N을/를 타고 가다/오다

'타고 가다/오다' is used to show by what mode of transportation one goes/comes to a place. To simply express what mode of transportation is taken, use the verb '타다'. When expressing 'come/go on foot', the pattern

'걸어(서) 가다/오다' is used.

A : 집에 어떻게 가요?	How do you go home?
B : 버스를 타고 가요.	I go by bus.
A : 학교에 어떻게 와요?	How do you come to school?
B : 걸어서 와요.	I come (to school) on foot.

5. 'ㄷ' irregular verbs

'ㄷ' in 'ㄷ' irregular verbs such as '걷다', '듣다' changes into 'ㄹ' when combined with the ending beginning with vowels as in '걸어요' and '들어요'.

-아요/어요 걷다 → 걸어요
듣다 → 들어요

-았어요/었어요 걷다 → 걸었어요
듣다 → 들었어요

-(으)ㄹ 거예요 걷다 → 걸을 거예요
듣다 → 들을 거예요

-(으)세요 걷다 → 걸으세요
듣다 → 들으세요

-지만 걷다 → 걷지만
듣다 → 듣지만

6. V-아야/어야 되다

'-아야/어야 되다' means 'should', 'ought to' or 'must'.

If the verb stem's last vowel ends with 'ㅏ' or 'ㅗ' + -아야 돼요 : 가다 → 가야 돼요
If the verb ends with '하다', 하다 → 해야 돼요 : 공부하다 → 공부해야 돼요
In all other cases, add '-어야 돼요' : 읽다 → 읽어야 돼요

-아야 돼요 사다 → 사야 돼요
가다 → 가야 돼요
타다 → 타야 돼요
만나다 → 만나야 돼요
보다 → 봐야 돼요
오다 → 와야 돼요

-해야 돼요 하다 → 해야 돼요
공부하다 → 공부해야 돼요
일하다 → 일해야 돼요
운동하다 → 운동해야 돼요
청소하다 → 청소해야 돼요
빨래하다 → 빨래해야 돼요

-어야 돼요 먹다 → 먹어야 돼요
입다 → 입어야 돼요
읽다 → 읽어야 돼요
마시다 → 마셔야 돼요
가르치다 → 가르쳐야 돼요
배우다 → 배워야 돼요

학교에 가야 돼요.	I should go to school.
한국어를 공부해야 돼요.	I should study Korean.
책을 읽어야 돼요.	I should read the book.

UNIT 3 Reason

1. 못 V

'못' followed by a verb means that one doesn't have the ability to do something or something is simply not possible.

'못 V' and '안 V' are different in meaning.

청소를 안 했어요. I didn't clean.
청소를 못 했어요. I couldn't clean.

오늘 학교에 못 가요.	I can't go to school today.
저는 피아노를 못 쳐요.	I can't play the piano.
어제 청소를 못 했어요.	I couldn't clean yesterday.

2. A/V-아서/어서

'-아서/어서' means 'because/since/so'. It is used to

connect two clauses. The first clause contains the reason for the following clause.

길이 복잡해요. + 지하철을 타요.
→ 길이 복잡해서 지하철을 타요.

If the verb or adjective stem's last vowel ends with 'ㅏ' or 'ㅗ' + -아서 : 비싸다 → 비싸서
If the verb or adjective ends with '하다', 하다 → 해서 : 복잡하다 → 복잡해서
In all other cases, add '-어서' : 있다 → 있어서

-아서	비싸다 → 비싸서 많다 → 많아서 오다 → 와서
-해서	복잡하다 → 복잡해서 일하다 → 일해서 피곤하다 → 피곤해서
-어서	있다 → 있어서 없다 → 없어서 마시다 → 마셔서

The verb or adjective of the preceding sentence takes only the basic form, and the tense is expressed in the sentence that follows.

비쌌어요. + 안 샀어요.
→ 비쌌어서 안 샀어요. (X)
→ 비싸서 안 샀어요. (O)

시험이 있어서 공부해야 돼요.
I should study since I have a test.

길이 복잡해서 지하철을 타요.
I take the subway because the traffic is heavy.

A : 왜 안 샀어요? Why didn't you buy?
B : 비싸서 안 샀어요. I didn't because it was expensive.

3. 'ㅂ' irregular adjectives

When adjectives whose stems end with 'ㅂ' meet the ending which begins with a vowel as '아/어' or '으', 'ㅂ' changes into '우'.

맵다 : 맵 + -어요 → 매워요
맵 + -어서 → 매워서

-아요/어요	덥다 → 더워요 맵다 → 매워요 춥다 → 추워요 쉽다 → 쉬워요 어렵다 → 어려워요 시끄럽다 → 시끄러워요
-았어요/었어요	덥다 → 더웠어요 맵다 → 매웠어요 춥다 → 추웠어요 쉽다 → 쉬웠어요 어렵다 → 어려웠어요 시끄럽다 → 시끄러웠어요
-아서/어서	덥다 → 더워서 맵다 → 매워서 춥다 → 추워서 쉽다 → 쉬워서 어렵다 → 어려워서 시끄럽다 → 시끄러워서
-지만	덥다 → 덥지만 맵다 → 맵지만 춥다 → 춥지만 쉽다 → 쉽지만 어렵다 → 어렵지만 시끄럽다 → 시끄럽지만

책이 어려워서 못 읽어요.
I can't read because the book is difficult.

A : 왜 김치를 안 먹어요? Why don't you eat kimchi?
B : 매워서 안 먹어요. I don't because it is spicy.

4. N(이)라서

Together with a noun, this pattern shows the reason for the sentence that follows.

휴가예요. + 회사에 안 가요.
→ 휴가라서 회사에 안 가요.

If the noun ends with a vowel + –라서 : 휴가 → 휴가라서
If the noun ends with a consonant + –이라서 :
외국 사람 → 외국 사람이라서

휴가라서 회사에 안 가요.
I don't go to work because I'm on my vacation.

그 사람은 외국 사람이라서 한국어를 못 해요.
(S)he can't speak Korean because (s)he is a foreigner.

A : 왜 케이크를 샀어요? Why did you buy a cake?
B : 친구 생일이라서 케이크를 샀어요.
I bought it because it is my friend's birthday.

5. N(이)나 N'

When suggesting two alternative nouns, '(이)나' is added to the first of the two choices to connect the two nouns.

If the noun ends with a vowel + 나 : 버스 → 버스나
If the noun ends with a consonant + 이나 :
토요일 → 토요일이나

버스나 지하철을 타고 가요.
I take the bus or subway.

토요일이나 일요일에 시간 있어요?
Do you have time on Saturday or Sunday?

UNIT 4 Post Office

1. V–(으)ㄹ 거예요

'–(으)ㄹ 거예요' indicates the subject's future plans or intentions.

If the verb stem ends with a vowel + –ㄹ 거예요 :
가다 → 갈 거예요
If the verb stem ends with a consonant + –을 거예요 :
읽다 → 읽을 거예요

내일 백화점에 갈 거예요.
I'm going to the department store tomorrow.

주말에 책을 읽을 거예요.
I will read books on the weekend.

A : 내일 뭘 할 거예요?
What are you going to do tomorrow?
B : 집에서 쉴 거예요. I am going to rest at home.

V–(으)실 거예요

'–(으)실 거예요' is a combination of '–(으)시–', which denotes respect towards the subject, and '–(으)ㄹ 거예요', which is a future tense sentence ending.

If the verb stem ends with a vowel + –실 거예요 :
가다 → 가실 거예요
If the verb stem ends with a consonant + –으실 거예요 :
입다 → 입으실 거예요

아버지는 내일 병원에 가실 거예요.
My father is going to the hospital tomorrow.

어머니는 내일 한복을 입으실 거예요.
My mother will wear hanbok tomorrow.

A : 선생님, 주말에 뭘 하실 거예요?
Sir/Ma'am, what are you going to do on the weekend?
B : 친구를 만날 거예요. I am going to meet my friend.

2. N(으)로

'(으)로' indicates the means or method.

If the noun ends with a vowel + 로 :
비행기 → 비행기로
If the noun ends with a consonant + 으로 :
젓가락 → 젓가락으로
If the noun ends with 'ㄹ' + '로' :
지하철 → 지하철로
연필 → 연필로

비행기로 보낼 거예요.	I will send it by airplane.
젓가락으로 냉면을 먹어요. I eat naengmyeon with chopsticks.	
지하철로 왔어요.	I took the subway here.

3. A/V-(으)면

'-(으)면' indicates conditions or assumptions.

If the verb or adjective stem ends with a vowel + -면 :
끝나다 → 끝나면
If the verb or adjective stem ends with a consonant + -으면 : 있다 → 있으면

시험이 끝나면 여행을 갈 거예요. When the test is over, I'm going to take a trip.
시간이 있으면 영화를 봐요. When I have time, I watch movies.
추우면 코트를 입으세요. If you're cold, put on a coat.

4. N한테

Adding '한테' to a person, denotes that he/she is the receiver of the action described.

친구한테 소포를 부쳤어요. I sent a parcel to a friend.
동생한테 전화해요. I am making a phone call to my younger brother/sister.
A : 누구한테 꽃을 줄 거예요? To whom are you going to give the flowers? B : 여자 친구한테 줄 거예요. I am going to give them to my girlfriend.

'에게' can be used instead of '한테' but '한테' is more conversational.

친구한테 = 친구에게

When the receiver of an action is a place, '에' is added.

미국에 소포를 부쳤어요.
회사에 전화해요.

UNIT 5 Reservations

1. V-(으)ㄹ 수 있다

'V-(으)ㄹ 수 있다' is used to express possibility or ability.

If the verb stem ends with a vowel + -ㄹ 수 있어요 :
치다 → 칠 수 있어요
If the verb stem ends with a consonant + -을 수 있어요 :
먹다 → 먹을 수 있어요

When express impossibility or inability '못 V' or 'V-(으)ㄹ 수 없다' are used.

못 쳐요. = 칠 수 없어요.
못 먹어요. = 먹을 수 없어요.

A : 테니스를 칠 수 있어요?	Can you play tennis?
B : 네, 칠 수 있어요.	Yes, I can.
아니요, 못 쳐요.	No, I can't.
A : 김치를 먹을 수 있어요?	Can you eat kimchi?
B : 네, 먹을 수 있어요.	Yes, I can.
아니요, 못 먹어요.	No, I can't.

2. A-(으)ㄴ데요/V-는데요

'-(으)ㄴ데요/는데요' is the sentence ending often used in spoken language. And it sounds more polite than '-아요/어요'. It is often used when the speaker has something to add or expects a certain response from the listener.
For adjectives, '-(으)ㄴ데요' is attached.

If the adjective stem ends with a vowel + -ㄴ데요 :
바쁘다 → 바쁜데요
If the adjective stem ends with a consonant + -은데요 :
작다 → 작은데요

And for verbs, '-는데요' is attached.
가다 → 가는데요
먹다 → 먹는데요

A-(으)ㄴ데요

바쁘다 → 바쁜데요
나쁘다 → 나쁜데요
싸다 → 싼데요
비싸다 → 비싼데요
작다 → 작은데요
춥다 → 추운데요

V-는데요

가다 → 가는데요
먹다 → 먹는데요
자다 → 자는데요
읽다 → 읽는데요
만나다 → 만나는데요
듣다 → 듣는데요

For adjectives ending in '있다' or '없다', '-는데요' is added, even though they are not verbs.

맛있다 → 맛있는데요
재미없다 → 재미없는데요

N인데요

With nouns, '-인데요' is used.

A : 미국 사람이지요?	Are you American?
B : 아니요, 캐나다 사람인데요.	No, I am Canadian.

3. V-고 싶다

'-고 싶다' is used to express the subject's hope.

뭘 마시고 싶어요?	What do you like to drink?
A : 뭘 먹고 싶어요?	What do you like to eat?
B : 한국 음식을 먹고 싶어요.	I like to have Korean food.

If you want to use a third person as a subject, you have to use the 'V-고 싶어하다' pattern instead of 'V-고 싶다'.

애니 씨는 커피를 마시고 싶어해요.

4. N 동안

'동안' denotes the duration of an event or state.

한 시간 동안
삼 일 동안
일주일 동안
한 달 동안
일 년 동안
방학 동안

내일부터 일주일 동안 미국을 여행할 거예요.
From tomorrow I am going to travel around the U.S. for a week.

A : 얼마 동안 계실 거예요?
For how long are you going to stay?
B : 삼일 동안 있을 거예요.
I am going to stay for three days.

5. N부터

Together with time-related words such as hour, date, day, etc., '부터' shows the beginning point of time and '까지' indicates the ending point.

6시부터 9시까지
12일부터 15일까지
월요일부터 금요일까지
어제부터 내일까지

9시부터 5시까지 회사에서 일해요.
I work from 9 a.m. to 5 p.m.

어제부터 집에서 쉬었어요.
I have been resting at home since yesterday.

UNIT 6 Etiquette

1. V-아도/어도 되다

'-아도/어도 되다' is used to express permission. In a question, this pattern is used to ask permission from another person. In a declarative sentence, it expresses the permission of the speaker.

If the verb stem's last vowel ends with 'ㅏ' or 'ㅗ' + –아도 돼요 : 가다 → 가도 돼요
If the verb ends with '하다', 하다 → 해도 돼요 : 전화하다 → 전화해도 돼요
In all other cases, add '–어도 돼요' : 먹다 → 먹어도 돼요

–아도 돼요	가다 → 가도 돼요 사다 → 사도 돼요 닫다 → 닫아도 돼요
–해도 돼요	하다 → 해도 돼요 전화하다 → 전화해도 돼요 수영하다 → 수영해도 돼요
–어도 돼요	먹다 → 먹어도 돼요 피우다 → 피워도 돼요 마시다 → 마셔도 돼요

A : 집에 가도 돼요?	May I go home?
B : 네, 가도 돼요.	Yes, you may.
A : 밤에 전화해도 돼요?	May I call you at night?
B : 네, 전화해도 돼요.	Yes, you may.
A : 담배를 피워도 돼요?	May I smoke?
B : 네, 피워도 돼요.	Yes, you may.

'–아도/어도 괜찮다' can be used instead of '–아도/어도 되다'.

담배를 피워도 돼요?

2. V–(으)면 안 되다

'–(으)면 안 되다' is used to express prohibition.

If the verb stem ends with a vowel + –면 안 돼요 : 가다 → 가면 안 돼요
If the verb stem ends with a consonant + –으면 안 돼요 : 먹다 → 먹으면 안 돼요

집에 가면 안 돼요.	You may not go home.
이 빵을 먹으면 안 돼요.	You may not eat this bread.

3. A/V–(으)ㄹ 때

You can use '–(으)ㄹ 때' to describe general occasions.

If the verb or adjective stem ends with a vowel + –ㄹ 때 : 들어가다 → 들어갈 때
If the verb or adjective stem ends with a consonant + –을 때 : 먹다 → 먹을 때

한국에서는 집에 들어갈 때 신발을 벗어요. In Korea when going into a house, we take off our shoes.
밥을 먹을 때 이야기하면 안 돼요. When you eat, you shouldn't talk.

UNIT 7 Hospital

1. 'ㅡ' irregular verbs & adjectives

When verbs and adjectives with vowel ending 'ㅡ' in their stem meet '–아/어–', 'ㅡ' is dropped and '–아–' or '–어–' is added.
'–아–' is added when the stem has either 'ㅏ' or 'ㅗ', as in the following examples.

바쁘다 : 바쁘 + –아요 → 바빠요
배고프다 : 배고프 + –아서 → 배고파서

In other cases, '–어–' is added.

예쁘다 : 예쁘 + –어요 → 예뻐요
쓰다 : 쓰 + –어서 → 써서

–아요/어요	바쁘다 → 바빠요 아프다 → 아파요 배고프다 → 배고파요 예쁘다 → 예뻐요 쓰다 → 써요 크다 → 커요
–았어요/었어요	바쁘다 → 바빴어요 아프다 → 아팠어요 배고프다 → 배고팠어요 예쁘다 → 예뻤어요

Grammar Reference 문법 설명

쓰다 → 썼어요
크다 → 컸어요

–아서/어서	바쁘다 → 바빠서 아프다 → 아파서 배고프다 → 배고파서 예쁘다 → 예뻐서 쓰다 → 써서 크다 → 커서
–(으)면	바쁘다 → 바쁘면 아프다 → 아프면 배고프다 → 배고프면 예쁘다 → 예쁘면 쓰다 → 쓰면 크다 → 크면

내일 바빠요.	I'm busy tomorrow.
너무 배고파요.	I'm so hungry.
애니 씨는 예뻐요.	Annie is pretty.
저는 매일 일기를 써요.	I keep a diary everyday.

2. N이/가 아프다

When expressing where you feel the pain, '이/가 아프다' is added to the part of body.

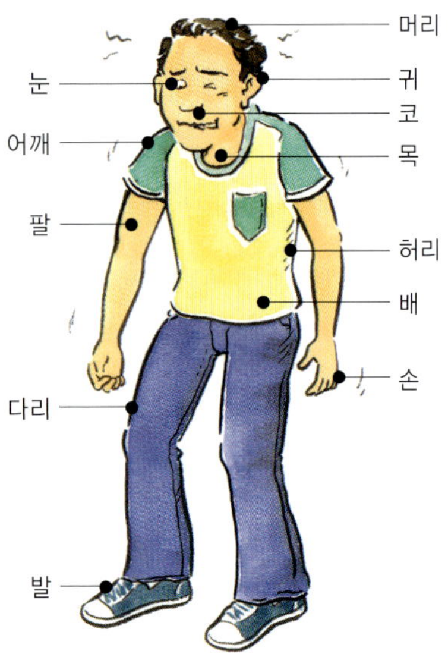

A : 어디가 아파요?	Where does it hurt?
B : 머리가 아파요.	My head hurts.

목이 아파서 병원에 갔어요.
I went to the clinic because my throat hurt.

3. N도

'도' is used to express the meaning of 'also'. When '도' is used after a subject or an object, subject particle and object particle(이/가, 을/를…) are not used with '도', but only '도' is used.

영준 씨가도 학교에 왔어요. (X)
영준 씨도 학교에 왔어요. (O)

A : 어디가 아파요? Where does it hurt?
B : 머리가 아파요. 그리고 배도 아파요.
I have a headache and I have a stomachache, too.

A : 어제 뭘 샀어요?
What did you buy yesterday?
B : 옷을 샀어요. 그리고 구두도 샀어요.
I bought some clothes and I bought shoes, too.

4. A/V–(으)니까

'–(으)니까' means 'because', 'since' or 'so'.

If the verb or adjective stem ends with a vowel + –니까 : 보다 → 보니까
If the verb or adjective stem ends with a consonant +–으니까 : 먹다 → 먹으니까

There is an important difference between '–아서/어서' and '–(으)니까'. When expressing the conditions or reasons for an order or a suggestion, '–아서/어서' can not be used. (refer to ☞ unit 3)

날씨가 좋아서 산에 갈까요? (X)
→ 날씨가 좋으니까 산에 갈까요? (O)

오늘은 바쁘니까 내일 오세요.
Since I'm busy today, please come tomorrow.

날씨가 좋으니까 산에 갈까요?
Since the weather is nice, shall we go to the mountains?

When the tense of the preceding sentence is past, 'A/V-았/었으니까' form is used.

술을 마셨어요. + 운전하지 마세요.
→ 술을 마셨으니까 운전하지 마세요.

5. V-지 마세요

'-지 마세요' is the negative imperative form.

가다 → 가지 마세요
앉다 → 앉지 마세요

날씨가 추우니까 밖에 나가지 마세요.
Since it is cold, please don't go outside.

여기에서 담배를 피우지 마세요.
Do not smoke here.

UNIT 8 Advice & Suggestions

1. N은/는 N′한테 좋다/나쁘다

This expression means that N is good/bad for N′. When N′ is a person or an animal, '한테' is used after N′. In written Korean, usually '에게' is used rather than '한테'.

이 운동은 여자들한테 좋아요.
This exercise is beneficial to women.

커피는 아이들에게 나빠요. Coffee is bad for children.

2. N은/는 N′에 좋다/나쁘다

This expression means that N is good/bad for N′.

When N′ is an inanimated thing, '에' is used after N′.

오렌지 주스는 감기에 좋아요.
Orange juice is good for cold.

담배는 몸에 나빠요. Cigarettes are bad for your health.

3. V-아/어 보세요

'V-아/어 보세요' is a sentence ending denoting a suggestion or recommendation. This can be used when politely inducing someone to try something.

If the verb stem's final vowel ends with 'ㅏ' or 'ㅗ' + -아 보세요 : 가다 → 가 보세요
If the verb ends with '하다', 하다 → 해 보세요 :
전화하다 → 전화해 보세요
In all other cases, add '-어 보세요' : 먹다 → 먹어 보세요

-아 보세요
가다 → 가 보세요
사다 → 사 보세요
타다 → 타 보세요
만나다 → 만나 보세요
오다 → 와 보세요

-해 보세요
하다 → 해 보세요
수영하다 → 수영해 보세요
일하다 → 일해 보세요
운동하다 → 운동해 보세요
공부하다 → 공부해 보세요

-어 보세요
먹다 → 먹어 보세요
입다 → 입어 보세요
마시다 → 마셔 보세요
가르치다 → 가르쳐 보세요
배우다 → 배워 보세요

A : 감기에 걸렸어요. I caught a cold.
B : 병원에 가 보세요.
Why don't you go to the hospital?

A : 요즘 살이 많이 쪘어요.
I gained a lot of weight these days.
B : 수영을 해 보세요. Try swimming.

A : 머리가 아파요. I have a headache.
B : 이 약을 한번 먹어 보세요. Try this medicine.

'V-아/어 보세요' usually comes with '한번'.
이 약을 한번 먹어 보세요.

4. V-는 게 어때요?

'V-는 게 어때요?' is used when suggesting something.

A : 요즘 살이 많이 쪘어요.
I gained a lot of weight these days.
B : 운동하는 게 어때요?
How about doing some excercise?

A : 감기에 걸려서 머리가 아파요.
I have a headache because I caught a cold.
B : 약을 먹는 게 어때요?
Why don't you take medicine?

5. 'ㄹ' irregular verbs & adjectives

When a verb or adjective stem ends in 'ㄹ' is followed by endings beginning with 'ㄴ', 'ㅂ', or 'ㅅ', the stem's 'ㄹ' is dropped. And also in this case, '-(으)' which is supposed to be added to the stem with consonant ending is also dropped.

-(으)세요
만들다 → 만드세요
살다 → 사세요
알다 → 아세요

-(으)ㄴ/는데요
만들다 → 만드는데요
살다 → 사는데요
알다 → 아는데요
멀다 → 먼데요
길다 → 긴데요

-(으)니까
만들다 → 만드니까
살다 → 사니까
알다 → 아니까
멀다 → 머니까
길다 → 기니까

-(으)면
만들다 → 만들면
살다 → 살면
알다 → 알면
멀다 → 멀면
길다 → 길면

-아요/어요
만들다 → 만들어요
살다 → 살아요
알다 → 알아요
멀다 → 멀어요
길다 → 길어요

-지만
만들다 → 만들지만
살다 → 살지만
알다 → 알지만
멀다 → 멀지만
길다 → 길지만

학교 옆에 사니까 아주 좋아요.
It is really good to be living near the school.

미영 씨 전화번호를 알면 가르쳐 주세요.
If you know Miyeong's phone number, please tell me.

A : 지금 뭐 해요? What are you doing now?
B : 불고기를 만드는데요. I am making bulgogi.

UNIT 9 Shopping

1. A-(으)ㄴ N

By adding '-(으)ㄴ' to an adjective stem and placing it in front of a noun, the adjective modifies and defines the state or characteristic of the noun.

If the adjective stem ends with a vowel + -ㄴ :
예쁘다 + 옷 → 예쁜 옷
If the adjective stem ends with a consonant + -은 :
좋다 + 약 → 좋은 약

A-(으)ㄴ	
	크다 → 큰
	싸다 → 싼
	예쁘다 → 예쁜
	편하다 → 편한
	작다 → 작은
	높다 → 높은
	낮다 → 낮은
	좋다 → 좋은
	쉽다 → 쉬운
	어렵다 → 어려운
	길다 → 긴
	힘들다 → 힘든

예쁜 옷을 사고 싶어요.
I'd like to buy some pretty clothes.

저는 착한 사람이 좋아요. I like good-natured people.

However, when the adjectives end in 있다 or 없다 such as 재미있다 and 재미없다, it modifies the noun with the ending '-는', not '-(으)ㄴ'.

맛있다 → 맛있는
재미없다 → 재미없는

맛있는 음식을 먹고 싶어요.
I want to eat delicious food.

어떤

When asking about the characteristics, special qualities and contents of a thing, person, work, etc., '어떤' is added to the thing.

A : 어떤 음식을 좋아해요?
What kind of food do you like?
B : 저는 매운 음식을 좋아해요. I like spicy food.

Compare to '무슨'. (refer to ☞ unit 1)

A : 어떤 영화를 보고 싶어요?
B : 무서운 영화를 보고 싶어요.
A : 무슨 영화를 보고 싶어요?
B : '집으로'를 보고 싶어요.

2. S-고 S'

By using '-고' after a verb or adjective stem of first clause, two sentences of an equal status, which are enumerated using '그리고', can be combined into one.

이 치마는 싸요. 그리고 예뻐요.
= 이 치마는 싸고 예뻐요.

나는 학교에 가요. 그리고 형은 회사에 가요.
= 나는 학교에 가고 형은 회사에 가요.

The tense is only expressed in the final sentence ending.

어제 텔레비전을 봤어요. 그리고 숙제를 했어요.
= 어제 텔레비전을 보고 숙제를 했어요.

이 치마는 싸고 예뻐요.
This skirt is cheap and pretty.

나는 학교에 가고 형은 회사에 가요.
I go to school and my elder brother works for a company.

어제 텔레비전을 보고 숙제를 했어요.
I watched television and did homework yesterday.

3. N을/를 N'(으)로 바꾸다

When exchanging something for something else, use '을/를' with the preceding noun, and add '(으)로' to the following noun.

달러를 한국 돈으로 바꿨어요.

이거 좀 바꿔 주세요.	Exchange this please.
긴 치마로 바꿀 거예요.	I am going to exchange this for a long skirt.
A : 어떻게 오셨어요?	How can I help you?
B : 이십만 원을 달러로 바꾸고 싶은데요.	I'd like to exchange 200,000 won for dollar.

4. N보다 (더) A

When comparing two things, the particle '보다' is added to the one, which is the basis of the comparison, and '더' which means 'more', is added in front of adjective.

The order of the two objects compared could be flexibly changed with no change in meaning.

야구가 축구보다 더 재미있어요.
= 축구보다 야구가 더 재미있어요.

The adverb '더' can be omitted giving no change of meaning to the sentence.

오늘이 어제보다 더 바빠요.
= 오늘이 어제보다 바빠요.

서울이 부산보다 더 커요.	Seoul is bigger than Busan.
축구보다 야구가 더 재미있어요.	Baseball is more interesting than soccer.
오늘이 어제보다 바빠요.	Today is busier than yesterday.

5. A-(으)ㄴ 거

When a thing is already mentioned in the previous sentence, it is alright to repeat it again, but it is also alright to replace it with '거'.

A : 어떤 음식을 좋아하세요?
B : 매운 음식을 좋아해요.
= 매운 거를 좋아해요.

'거' is not used alone and always comes after a modifying word and cannot be used to indicate a person or place.

In literary and formal situations, '것' is preferred to '거'.

비싼 거 → 비싼 것
재미있는 거 → 재미있는 것

A : 어떤 음식을 좋아하세요?	What kind of food do you like?
B : 매운 거 좋아해요.	I like spicy food.
그거보다 더 작은 거 주세요.	Give me a smaller one than that.

Listening Transcript 듣기 지문

UNIT 1 Family

p. 25

1. Listen to Yeongjun's talk and match each family member with their respective workplace.

우리 가족은 모두 여섯 명이에요. 아버지, 어머니, 누나, 형, 동생이 한 명 있어요. 아버지는 회사에 다니세요. 어머니는 간호사세요. 누나는 백화점에서 일해요. 그리고 형은 은행에 다녀요. 동생은 대학생이에요.

2. Write down Andy's sister's and brother's job.

여자 : 앤디 씨, 동생이 있어요?
앤디 : 네, 여동생이 한 명, 남동생이 한 명 있어요.
여자 : 앤디 씨의 여동생은 학생이에요?
앤디 : 아니요, 회사원이에요.
여자 : 남동생은 무슨 일을 해요?
앤디 : 학생이에요.

3. Listen to the dialogue and choose the correct photo they are talking about.

1) 여자 : 마이클 씨의 가족사진이에요?
마이클 : 네, 맞아요. 이 사람이 제 아내예요.
여자 : 정말 예쁘세요. 부인은 무슨 일을 하세요?
마이클 : 학교 선생님이에요.
여자 : 이 아이가 마이클 씨 딸이지요?
마이클 : 네, 우리 딸이에요.

2) 남자 : 웨이 씨, 뭘 보고 있어요?
웨이 : 가족사진을 보고 있어요.
남자 : 이분이 웨이 씨 어머니세요?
웨이 : 네, 우리 어머니세요.
남자 : 이 사람은 누구예요?
웨이 : 우리 언니예요.
남자 : 웨이 씨는 동생이 없어요?
웨이 : 네, 없어요.

UNIT 2 Transportation

p. 40

1. Listen carefully and match each place with the correct subway station.

1) 남자 : 명동에 어떻게 가야 돼요?
여자 : 지하철 4호선을 타고 명동역에서 내리세요.

2) 남자 : 애니 씨 집에 어떻게 가야 돼요?
여자 : 지하철 2호선을 타고 잠실역에서 내리세요.

3) 남자 : 한국대학교에 어떻게 가야 돼요?
여자 : 지하철 3호선을 타고 안국역에서 내리세요.

4) 남자 : 서울시장에 어떻게 가야 돼요?
여자 : 지하철 2호선을 타고 동대문운동장역에서 내리세요.

5) 남자 : 하나극장에 어떻게 가야 돼요?
여자 : 지하철 2호선을 타고 삼성역에서 내리세요.

2. What should he do? Match each name with the correct picture.

1) 애니 : 여보세요. 마이클 씨? 저 애니예요. 내일 같이 산에 갈까요?
마이클 : 월요일에 시험이 있어요. 공부해야 돼요.

2) 애니 : 여보세요. 영준 씨? 저 애니예요. 내일 같이 산에 갈까요?
영준 : 미안해요. 병원에 가야 돼요.

3) 애니 : 여보세요. 앤디 씨? 저 애니예요. 내일 같이 산에 갈까요?
앤디 : 시간이 없어요. 수영을 배워야 돼요.

4) 애니 : 여보세요. 토니 씨? 저 애니예요. 내일 같이 산에 갈까요?
토니 : 내일 여자 친구를 만나야 돼요.

3. Listen carefully and match.

1) 애니　: 마이클 씨, 어디에 가요?
마이클 : 병원에 가요.
애니　: 병원에 어떻게 가요?
마이클 : 지하철을 타고 가요.
애니　: 여기에서 병원까지 얼마나 걸려요?
마이클 : 30분쯤 걸려요.

2) 애니　: 크리스 씨, 어디에 가요?
크리스 : 시장에 가요.
애니　: 시장에 걸어서 가요?
크리스 : 아니요, 시간이 없어서 택시 타고 가요.
애니　: 여기에서 시장까지 얼마나 걸려요?
크리스 : 10분쯤 걸려요.

3) 영준　: 미사코 씨, 어디에 가요?
미사코 : 백화점에 가요.
영준　: 백화점에 어떻게 가요?
미사코 : 버스를 타고 가요.
영준　: 여기에서 백화점까지 얼마나 걸려요?
미사코 : 1시간쯤 걸려요.

UNIT 3 Reason

p. 53

1. Listen carefully and connect each person with the correct picture expressing the reason why the person couldn't go.

1) 여자　: 영준 씨, 내일 같이 산에 갈까요?
영준　: 내일요? 내일은 친구가 한국에 와서 공항에 가야 돼요.

2) 여자　: 라주 씨, 일요일에 수영장에 갈까요?
라주　: 미안해요. 월요일에 시험이 있어서 공부해야 돼요.

3) 여자　: 크리스 씨, 우리 백화점에 갈까요?
크리스 : 미안해요. 오늘 좀 피곤해서 집에서 쉬고 싶어요.

2. Listen to the dialogue and choose the correct answer.

남자 : 애니 씨, 이 영화 봤어요?
애니 : 아니요, 극장에 갔지만 표가 없어서 못 봤어요.
남자 : 그럼 이번 토요일에 같이 극장에 갈까요?
애니 : 토요일요? 토요일에는 일이 있어서 못 가요.
남자 : 그럼 일요일에는 어때요?
애니 : 좋아요.

(1) 애니 씨는 왜 이 영화를 못 봤어요?
(2) 두 사람은 언제 이 영화를 봐요?

3. Listen to the dialogue and mark O for True, and mark X for False.

Waitress : 뭐 드릴까요?
남자　: 뭐가 맛있어요?
Waitress : 불고기가 맛있어요.
남자　: 아, 저는 고기를 못 먹어요.
Waitress : 그럼 김밥이나 비빔밥은 어때요? 안에 고기가 안 들었어요.
남자　: 그래요? 그럼 비빔밥 주세요.

UNIT 4 Post Office

p. 65

1. Listen carefully and connect the pictures on the left with corresponding pictures on the right.

1) 비가 오면 집에서 텔레비전을 볼 거예요.
2) 날씨가 나쁘면 집에서 잘 거예요.
3) 돈이 없으면 집에서 밥을 먹을 거예요.
4) 약속이 없으면 집에서 컴퓨터를 할 거예요.

2. Listen carefully and choose the correct answer.

남자 : 이 소포를 부치고 싶어요.
여자 : 어디로 보내실 거예요?
남자 : 중국으로요.
여자 : 안에 뭐가 들었어요?

남자 : 옷이 들었어요. 중국까지 얼마나 걸려요?
여자 : 비행기로 보내면 1주일쯤 걸려요. 그리고 배로 보내면 한 달쯤 걸려요.
남자 : 비행기로 좀 부쳐 주세요. 얼마예요?
여자 : 잠깐만요. 18,000원이에요.
남자 : 여기 있어요.

1) 남자는 어디에 소포를 보냈어요?
2) 남자는 소포를 뭐로 보냈어요? 쓰세요.

3. Listen carefully and choose the correct answer.

여자 : 라주 씨, 이거 뭐예요?
라주 : 옷이에요. 동생 생일이라서 동생한테 보낼 거예요.
여자 : 그래요? 동생 생일이 언제예요?
라주 : 1월 15일이에요. 시간이 없어서 빨리 소포를 보내야 돼요.
여자 : 괜찮아요. 비행기로 보내면 동생이 15일쯤 받을 거예요.

1) 소포 안에 뭐가 들었어요?
2) 라주 씨는 누구한테 소포를 보낼 거예요?

UNIT 5 Reservations

p. 78

1. Listen carefully and check(√) on the things the person wants to do.

남자 : 방학에 뭘 하고 싶어요?
여자 : 일본어를 배우고 싶어요.
남자 : 그래요? 운동은 안 할 거예요?
여자 : 수영을 배우고 싶어요.
남자 : 여행은 안 가요?
여자 : 저는 여행을 안 좋아해요.
남자 : 주말에 산에 갈 거예요?
여자 : 피곤해서 쉬고 싶어요.

2. Listen carefully and fill in the blanks with the information.

1) 남자 : 파리 가는 비행기 표를 예약하고 싶은데요.
여자 : 언제 출발하실 거예요?
남자 : 2월 15일에 출발할 거예요. 아침 9시쯤에 비행기가 있어요?
여자 : 9시 30분 비행기가 있어요.
남자 : 요금이 어떻게 돼요?
여자 : 150만 원이에요.

2) 남자 : 6월 3일에 방콕에 가고 싶은데요.
여자 : 몇 시에 출발하실 거예요?
남자 : 오후 2시쯤요.
여자 : 죄송합니다. 오후 2시 비행기는 자리가 없는데요. 3시 20분 비행기에는 자리가 있어요.
남자 : 그럼 3시 20분 비행기를 예약해 주세요. 요금이 어떻게 돼요?
여자 : 37만 원이에요.

3) 남자 : 뉴욕에 가고 싶은데요.
여자 : 언제 출발하실 거예요?
남자 : 9월 23일요. 아침 비행기가 있어요?
여자 : 아침 7시 10분 비행기가 있는데요.
남자 : 그 비행기는 요금이 어떻게 돼요?
여자 : 190만 원이에요.
남자 : 그럼 그 비행기를 예약해 주세요.

3. Listen carefully and mark O for True, and mark X for False.

남자 : 방을 예약하고 싶은데요.
여자 : 네. 언제부터 계실 거예요?
남자 : 6월 5일부터 7일까지 있을 거예요.
여자 : 침대 방하고 온돌방이 있는데요.
남자 : 온돌방을 주세요. 요금이 어떻게 돼요?
여자 : 하루에 10만 원이에요. 성함이 어떻게 되세요?
남자 : 김영준이에요.

UNIT 6 Etiquette

p. 91

1. What shouldn't he do? Connect with the right sign.

1) 여자 : 저기요.
남자 : 네?
여자 : 여기에서 모자를 쓰면 안 돼요. 뒷사람이 영화를 못 봐요.
남자 : 죄송합니다.

2) 여자 : 저기요.
남자 : 네?
여자 : 여기에서 이야기하면 안 돼요. 다른 사람들이 책을 못 읽어요.
남자 : 미안해요.

3) 여자 : 저기요.
남자 : 네?
여자 : 여기에서 사진 찍으면 안 돼요.
남자 : 그래요? 죄송합니다.

2. You are invited to a friend's house. Check(√) on what you may do.

남자 : 와, 음식이 정말 많아요! 사진을 찍어도 괜찮아요?
여자 : 그럼요.
남자 : 이 술을 마시고 싶은데요. 마셔도 돼요?
여자 : 네. 드세요.
남자 : 담배 좀 피워도 돼요?
여자 : 아기가 있어서 안 돼요.

3. Why shouldn't the person do the following? Listen and write down the number of the corresponding picture.

1) 남자 : 밖에서 수영해도 돼요?
여자 : 날씨가 추워서 안 돼요.

2) 남자 : 김치를 아이한테 줘도 돼요?
여자 : 아니요, 안 돼요. 매워서 못 먹어요.

3) 남자 : 이 전화를 사용해도 돼요?
여자 : 아니요, 요금이 너무 비싸서 안 돼요.

4) 남자 : 미영 씨! 내일 미영 씨 집에 가도 돼요?
여자 : 미안해요. 일이 많아서 안 돼요.

4. What does he do when he is in the following mood? Match the moods with the activities.

1) 여자 : 심심할 때 뭐 해요?
남자 : 심심할 때 영화를 봐요.

2) 여자 : 기분이 좋을 때는요?
남자 : 기분이 좋을 때는 친구들을 만나요.

3) 여자 : 그럼 기분이 안 좋을 때는 뭐 해요?
남자 : 집에서 쉬어요.

4) 여자 : 슬플 때는 뭐 해요?
남자 : 그럴 때는 노래를 해요.

UNIT 7 Hospital

p. 105

1. Listen carefully and find out what one should not do, and then connect with the corresponding picture.

1) 배가 아프니까 술을 마시지 마세요.
2) 지금은 길이 복잡하니까 버스를 타지 마세요.
3) 이 옷은 비싸니까 사지 마세요.
4) 추우니까 창문을 열지 마세요.
5) 감기에 걸렸으니까 산에 가지 마세요.

2. Listen carefully and write down the number which best describes the symptoms.

1) doctor : 어떻게 오셨어요?
patient : 눈이 아파서 왔어요.

2) doctor : 어디가 아프세요?
patient : 허리가 너무 아파요.
doctor : 언제부터 아팠어요?
patient : 한 달쯤 됐어요.

3) doctor : 어떻게 오셨어요?
patient : 기침을 많이 해요. 그리고 콧물이 나요.

3. Listen carefully and check(√) on the correct answer.

doctor : 어디가 아프세요?
patient : 열도 나고 기침도 많이 나서 왔어요.
doctor : '아' 해 보세요.
patient : 아.
doctor : 감기에 걸렸으니까 많이 쉬어야 돼요. 그리고 목이 아프니까 물을 많이 드세요.
patient : 네. 내일도 와야 돼요?
doctor : 네, 내일 다시 한번 오세요.

1) 남자는 왜 병원에 왔어요?
2) 남자는 뭘 해야 돼요?

UNIT 8 Advice & Suggestions

p. 118

1. Listen carefully and write down the number of the corresponding picture.

1) 남자 : 내일 뭘 할까요?
여자 : 영화를 보는 게 어때요?

2) 남자 : 머리가 아파요.
여자 : 병원에 가 보세요.

3) 남자 : 너무 피곤해요.
여자 : 좀 쉬는 게 어때요?

4) 남자 : 너무 추워요.
여자 : 창문을 닫는 게 어때요?

5) 남자 : 늦었어요.
여자 : 지하철을 타는 게 어때요?

2. Listen to the dialogue and choose the right answer.

남자 : 내일이 일요일인데 뭘 할까요?
여자 : 영화를 보는 게 어때요?
남자 : 글쎄요. 일요일에는 극장에 사람이 많으니까 산에 가는 게 어때요?
여자 : 좋아요.

두 사람은 내일 뭘 할 거예요?

3. Listen to the dialogue and choose the right answer.

여자 : 목이 너무 아파요.
남자 : 말을 많이 해서 그래요. 물을 많이 드셔 보세요. 목이 아프면 물을 많이 마셔야 돼요.

1) 여자는 어디가 아파요?
2) 여자는 뭘 해야 돼요?

4. Listen to the dialogue and choose the right answer.

여자 : 왜 그래요? 어디 아파요?
남자 : 점심을 너무 빨리 먹어서 배가 아파요.
여자 : 배가 아프면 이 약을 먹어 보세요.
남자 : 고마워요.

1) 남자는 왜 배가 아파요?
2) 남자는 어떻게 해야 돼요?

UNIT 9 Shopping

p. 131

1. Listen carefully and check(√) on the correct answer.

1) 호주가 일본보다 커요.
질문 : 어디가 더 커요?

2) 어제보다 오늘이 따뜻해요.
질문 : 언제 더 따뜻해요?

3) 주스가 커피보다 비싸요.
질문 : 뭐가 더 비싸요?

4) 토요일이 일요일보다 바빠요.
질문 : 언제 더 바빠요?

5) 사과보다 포도가 맛있어요.
질문 : 뭐가 더 맛있어요?

2. Listen carefully and choose the clothes purchased.

남자 : 뭘 찾으세요?
여자 : 하얀색 바지를 사고 싶은데요.
남자 : 이거 어떠세요?
여자 : 이거보다 짧은 바지를 좀 보여 주세요.
남자 : 그럼 이거 한번 입어 보세요. 어떠세요?
여자 : 아주 좋은데요. 이거 주세요. 그리고 저 파란색 티셔츠도 하나 주세요.

3. Listen to the following and mark O for True, and mark X for False.

저는 어제 남대문시장에 갔어요. 사람이 아주 많고 복잡했어요. 요즘 날씨가 추워서 코트를 사고 싶었어요. 빨간색 코트가 참 예뻤어요. 그렇지만 너무 비쌌어요. 그래서 코트를 안 사고 치마를 하나 샀어요. 옷을 사고 맛있는 비빔밥을 먹었어요. 참 재미있었어요. 다음에 또 가고 싶어요.

Glossary 찾아보기

ㄱ

		Unit
가족	family	1
간호사	nurse	1
갈색	brown	9
갈아타다	to transfer	2
감기	cold	7
같이	together	2
걱정	worry / concern	8
건강	health	8
걷다	to walk	2
결혼하다	to marry	1
결혼	marriage	5
경주	Gyeongju	2
계시다	to be / to stay (honorific)	5
고등학생	high school student	6
고민	agony / worry	8
고속터미널역	Express Bus Terminal Station	2
공	zero	5
공항	airport	3
괜찮다	alright	4
교대역	Seoul Nat'l Univ. of Education Station	2
귀	ear	7
그래서	so	7
그런데	but / by the way	6
그렇지만	but	8
그분	that person (honorific)	1
기분	feeling	6
기숙사	dormitory	6
기차표	train ticket	5
기차	train	2
기침	cough	7
기타	guitar	3
길다	long	8
까만색	black	9
깎다	to discount	9
꽃	flower	1
끝나다	to be finished	4
끝내다	to finish	3

ㄴ

		Unit
나다	to have (a fever/a runny nose)	7
나쁘다	bad	4
남대문시장	Namdaemun Market	2
남동생	younger brother	1
남부터미널역	Nambu Bus Terminal Station	2
남자	man / male	3
남편	husband	1
낮다	low	9
내	my	1
내다	to pay	8
내리다	to get off	2
너무	too	3
넘어지다	fall down	7
년	year	5
노란색	yellow	9
녹색	green	9
높다	high	9
누가	who	1
누구	who	1
누나	elder sister from a male perspective	1
눈	eye	7
눈	snow	4
눈사람	snowman	4
뉴스	news	3
뉴욕	New York	5

ㄷ

		Unit
다니다	to go to (a company) / to work for	1
다른	other	6
다리	leg	7
다음	next	9
다이어트	diet	8
다치다	to be hurt	7

달	month	4
달러	dollar	9
대학생	college student	1
덥다	hot	3
도서관	library	1
도와주다	to help	8
도착하다	to arrive	5
도쿄	Tokyo	5
동대문운동장역	Dongdaemun Stadium Station	2
동생	younger brother or sister	1
뒷사람	person behind	6
드라마	drama (TV series)	3
드시다	to eat (honorific)	6
듣다	to listen / to hear	2
-들	plural marker	3
들다	to be contained	3
들어가다	to go in / to enter	6
등산	mountain climbing / hiking	8
딸	daughter	1
땀	sweat	7
또	again / once more	9
똑똑하다	smart	9

ㄹ

		Unit
런던	London	5
로마	Rome	5
롯데월드	Lotte World	2

ㅁ

		Unit
마드리드	Madrid	5
많다	many / much	3
많이	many / much	3
말레이시아	Malaysia	4
말하기	speaking	8
맛없다	untasty	9
맞다	right	1
매일	everyday	7
맵다	hot and spicy	3
머리	head	7
멀다	far	8
명	counting unit for people	1
명동역	Myeongdong Station	2
명동	Myeong-dong	2
목	neck / throat	7
몸	body	7
무겁다	heavy	9
무섭다	scary	9
무슨	what	1
미안하다	sorry	3

ㅂ

		Unit
바꾸다	to exchange	9
바다	sea / ocean	5
바쁘다	busy	5
밖	outside	6
발	foot	7
방콕	Bangkok	5
방학	school holidays	5
배	abdomen / stomach	7
배고프다	hungry	4
배	ship / boat	2
버스	bus	2
번	counting unit after number	2
벗다	to take off	6
베이징	Beijing	5
베트남	Vietnam	4

Glossary 찾아보기

| ㅅ |

| ㅇ |

ㅈ

Unit

ㅊ

Unit

Glossary 찾아보기

| ㅋ |

| ㅌ |

| ㅍ |

| ㅎ |

집필위원

최은규 서울대학교 국어국문학과 박사
서울대학교 언어교육원 한국어교육센터 대우부교수

장은아 고려대학교 교육학과 박사
서울대학교 언어교육원 한국어교육센터 대우조교수

김은아 서울대학교 외국어교육과 박사과정 수료
서울대학교 언어교육원 한국어교육센터 대우조교수

채숙희 서울대학교 국어국문학과 박사
서울시립대학교 국제교육원 객원교수

남수경 서울대학교 국어국문학과 박사
서울대학교 인문학연구원 선임연구원

이숙현 시드니대학교 인문학부 석사
전 서울대학교 언어교육원 강사
모내시 대학교 한국학과 강사

Active Korean 2

지은이 서울대학교 언어교육원
발행처 (주)투판즈
주소 서울시 강남구 논현로 303
전화 (02)2140-2500
팩스 (02)2140-2599
인터넷 주소 www.twoponds.co.kr
등록 1980년 10월 7일 제2004-000086호
초판 1쇄 2007년 1월 10일
29쇄 2024년 8월 1일

「이 도서의 국립중앙도서관 출판시도서목록(CIP)은
e-CIP 홈페이지(http://www.nl.go.kr/ecip)에서 이용하실 수 있습니다.
(CIP제어번호: CIP2006002730)」